GANGSTA.

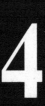

4

KOHSKE

THE HANDYMEN >

WORICK ARCANGELO

NICOLAS BROWN

< THEO'S CLINIC

DR. THEO

THE POLICE ⌄

ALEX BENEDETTO

NINA

CODY BALFOUR

CHAD ADKINS

CRISTIANO FAMILY >

MARCO ADRIANO

LORETTA CRISTIANO AMODIO

GALAHAD WOEHOR

STORY

GANGSTA._NO_004

2013020900004

In Ergastulum, a tough town run by the Mafia, the "Handymen" Nicolas and Worick make a living doing odd jobs for their clients, from routine deliveries to extrajudicial killings. The men are respected by both the police brass and the Mafia bosses, not least because Nicolas is a "Twilight," an ex-mercenary possessing extraordinary abilities. Now, as a new Twilight Hunt intensifies, Ergastulum is beginning to feel the pressure...

MONROE FAMILY >

YANG

DANIEL MONROE

DIEGO MONTES

MILES MAYER

DELICO

IVAN GLAZIEV

CORSICA FAMILY >

URANOS CORSICA

GINGER

DOUG

GINA PAULKLEE

^

PAULKLEE GUILD

CONTENTS

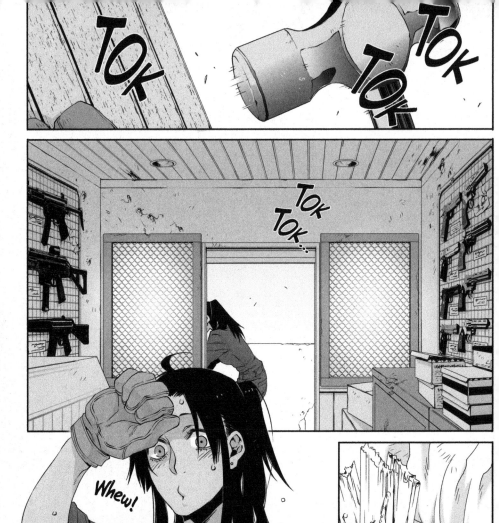

#17

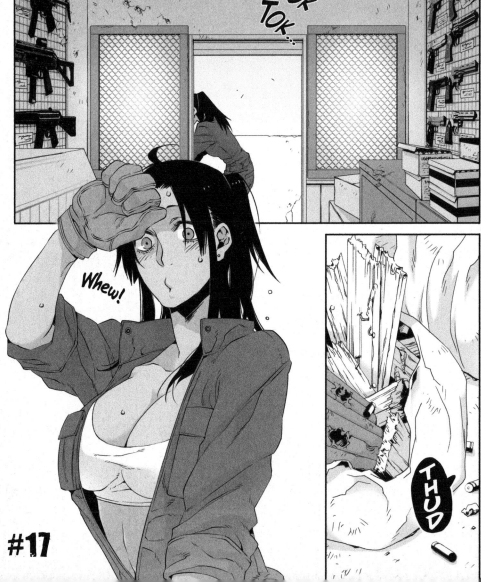

BUT—

IT'S OKAY, DON'T SWEAT IT.

TOK

TOK
TOK

HEY, ALEX!

YOU'VE DONE ENOUGH WORK FOR THE DAY.

COME AND HAVE SOME TEA!

PEEK

TOK
TOK

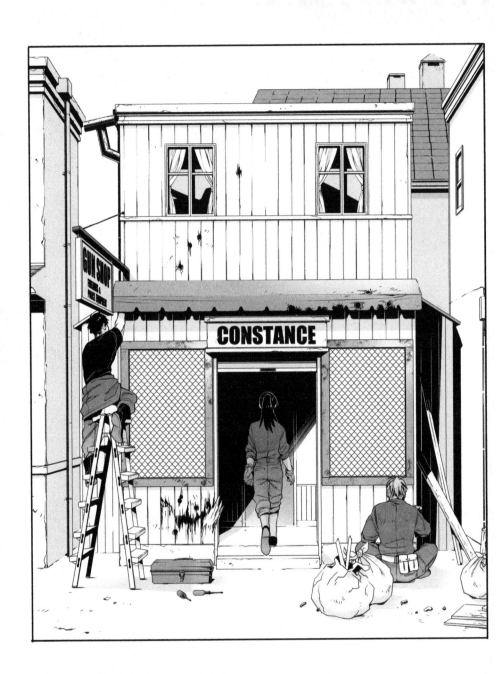

#17

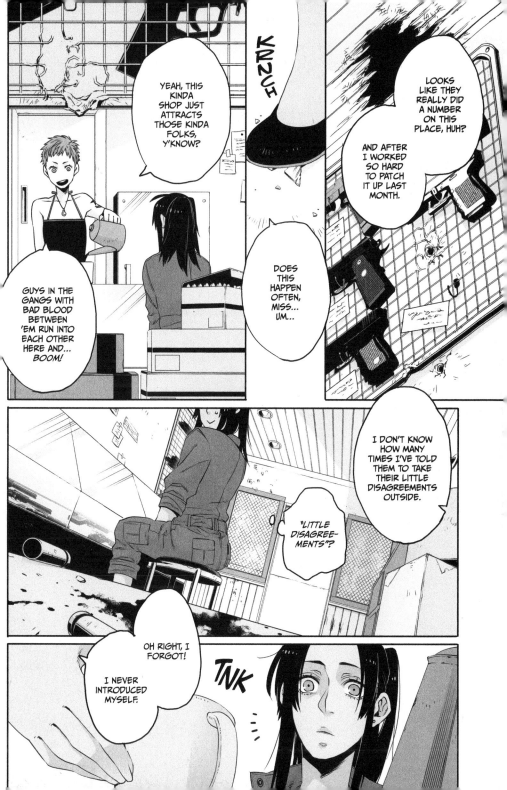

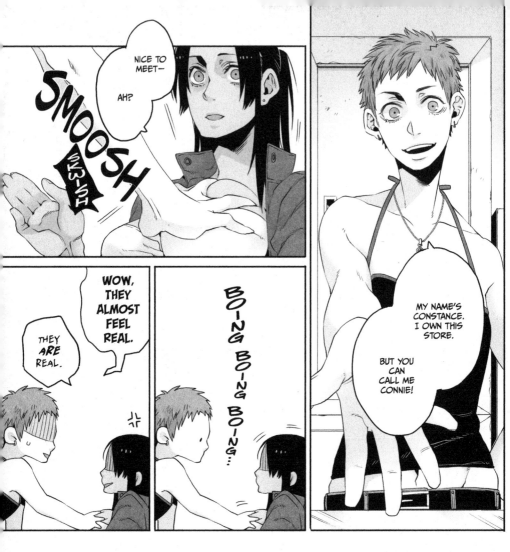
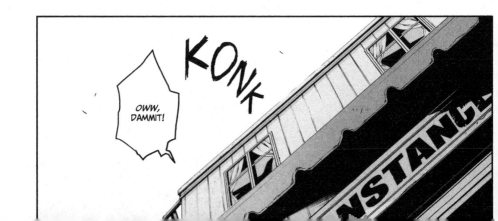

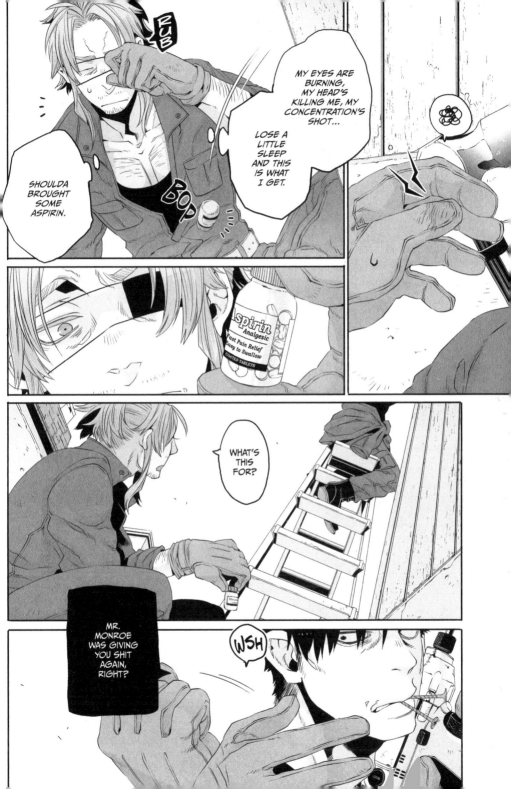

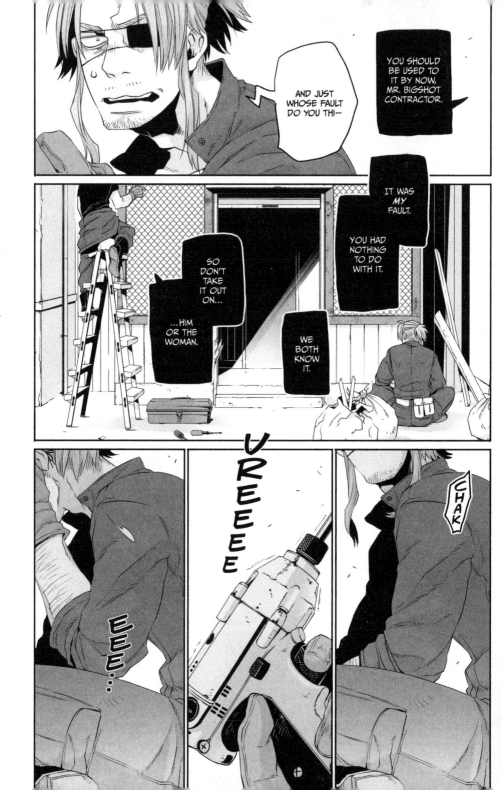

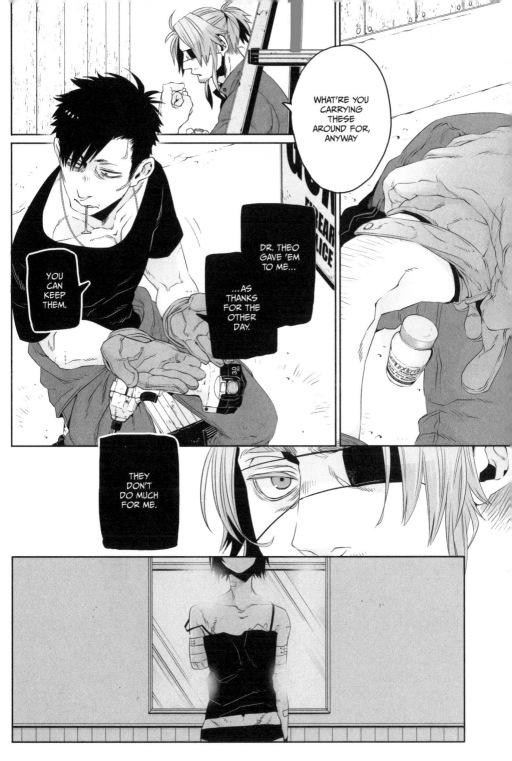

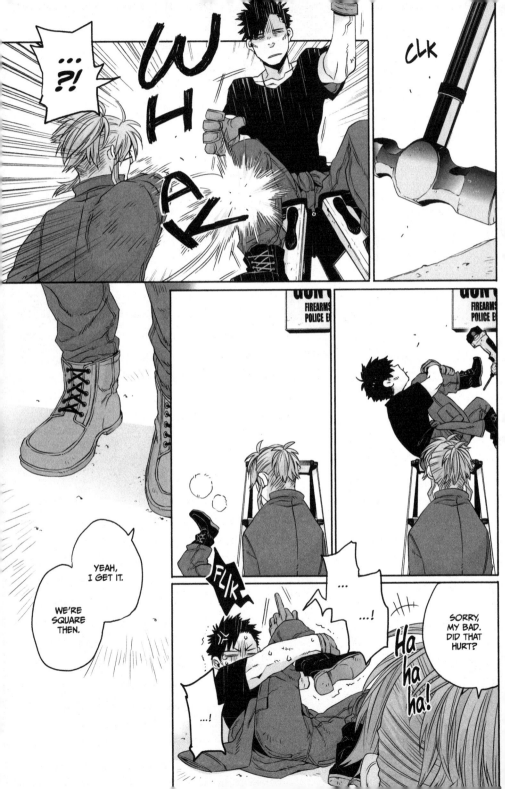

SHFL SHFL

I'M PAYING YOU, REMEMBER?

SO GET TO WORK.

AW, C'MON ON, GRANDMA JOEL!

HOLD IT RIGHT THERE, SONNY.

NO LAZING AROUND ON THE JOB.

YEEEOW!

POKE

HM? GRAMMY!

WHY DIDN'T YOU CALL? I COULD'VE PICKED YOU UP!

Bleh!

CRIK CRIK

...

OH, MY STARS...

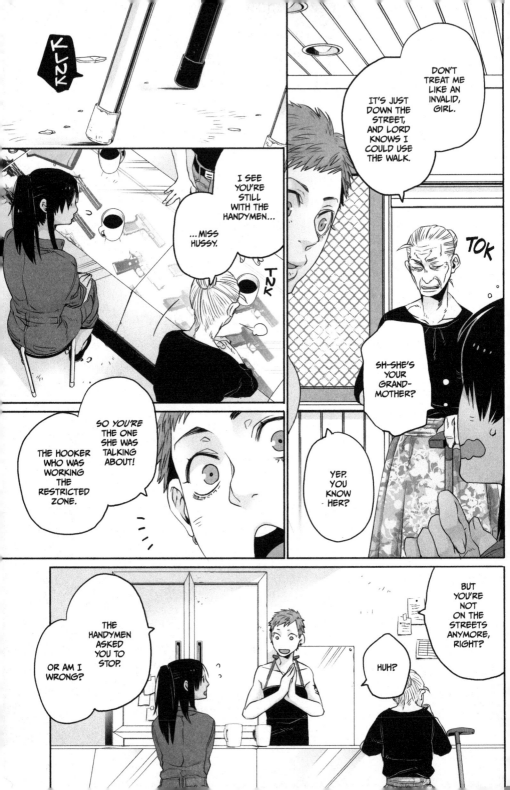

...GRAMMY IS JUST WORRIED ABOUT YOU. SHE'S AFRAID YOU'LL GET SOME PSYCHO JOHN AND—

OW, OW, OWIE!!

HMPH. YOU'LL BE BACK AT IT AGAIN BEFORE YOU KNOW IT.

I'VE SEEN IT HAPPEN TO A MILLION GIRLS.

UM, WELL...

IT MAY NOT SEEM LIKE IT BUT...

TUG

PSST

ANYWAY...

WHEN ARE YOU GOING TO GO HOME AND GET BACK TO YOUR FAMILY?

Ow!

MY STUPID GRAND-DAUGHTER NEEDS TO LEARN WHEN TO KEEP HER BIG MOUTH SHUT.

18

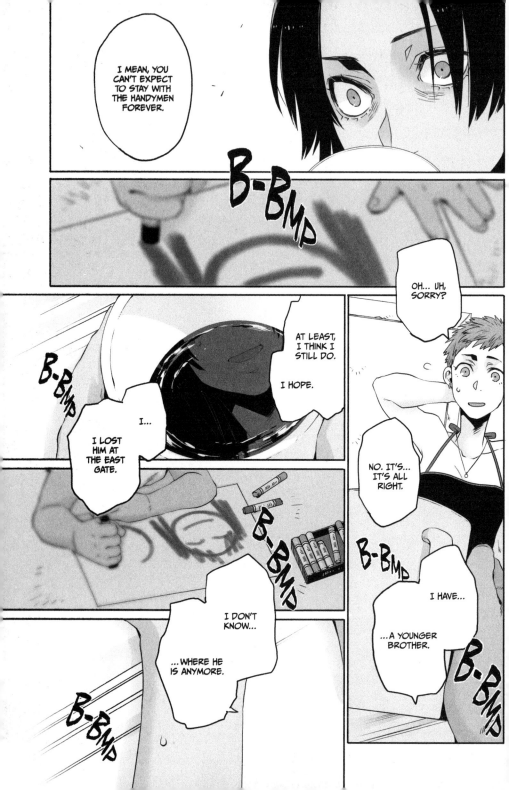

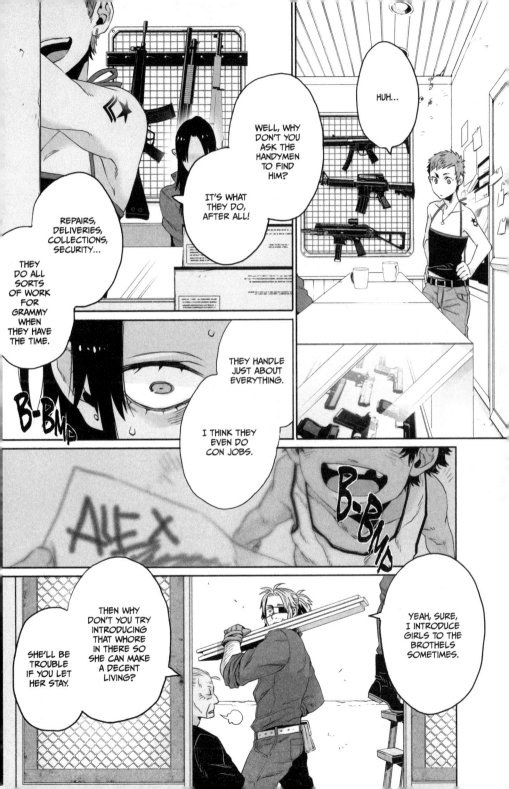

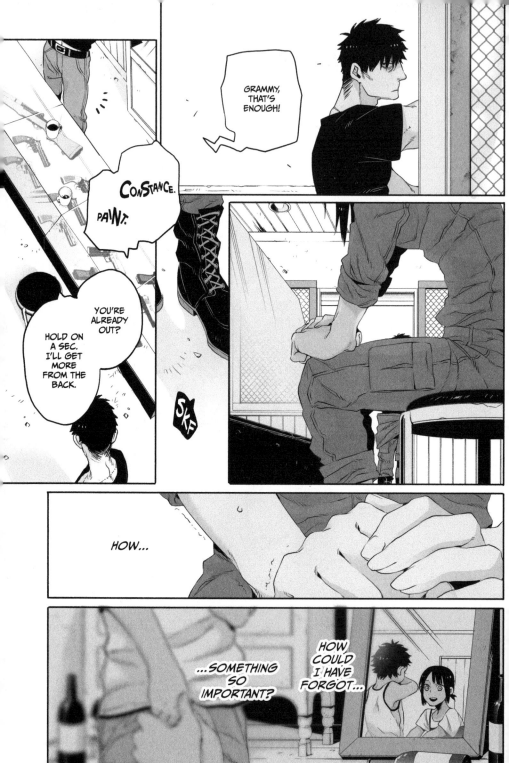

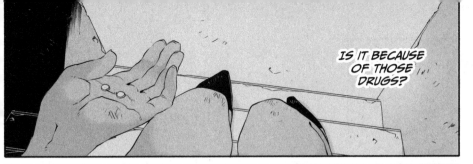

IS IT BECAUSE
OF THOSE
DRUGS?

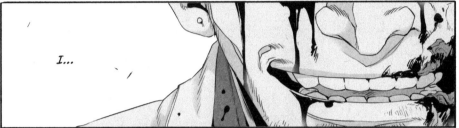

I...

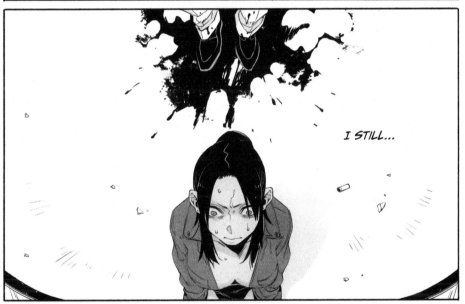

I STILL...

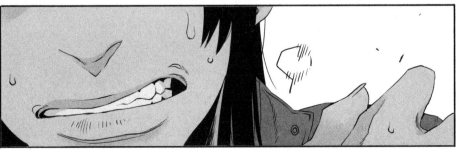

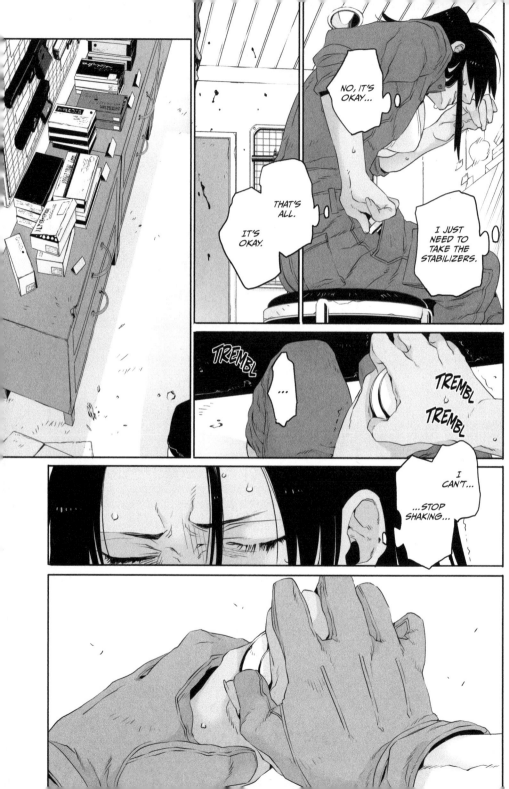

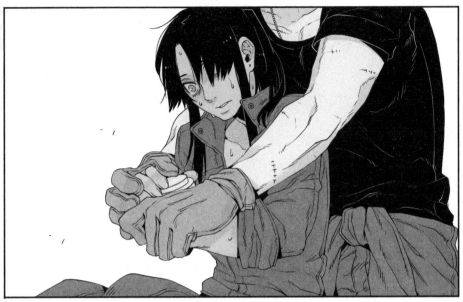

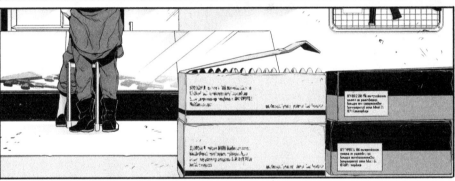

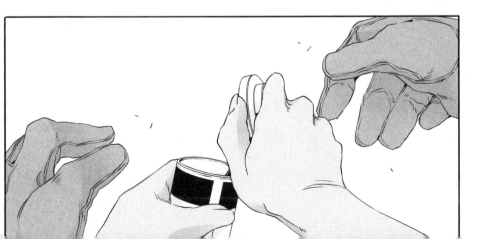

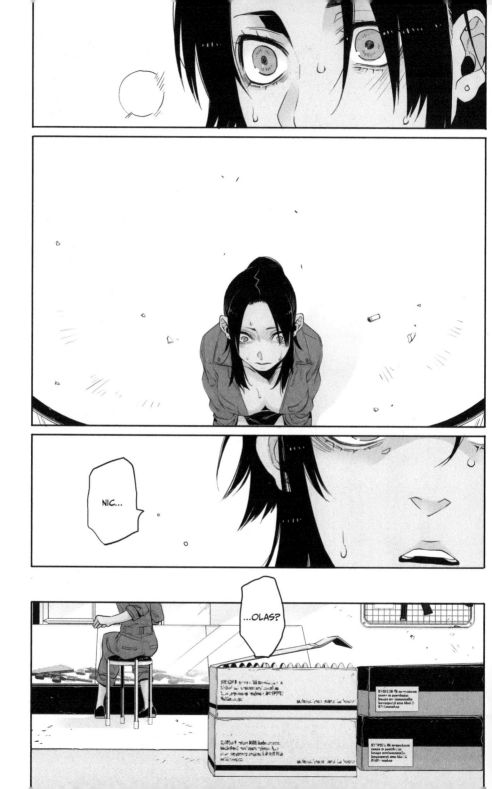

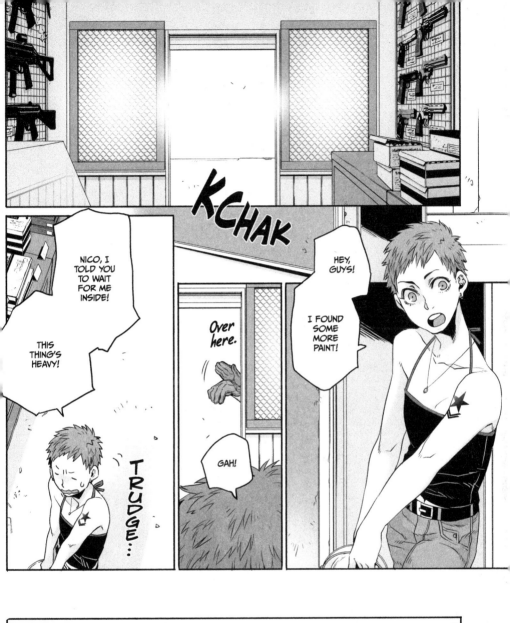

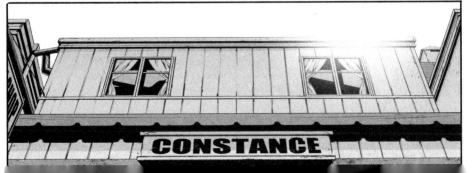

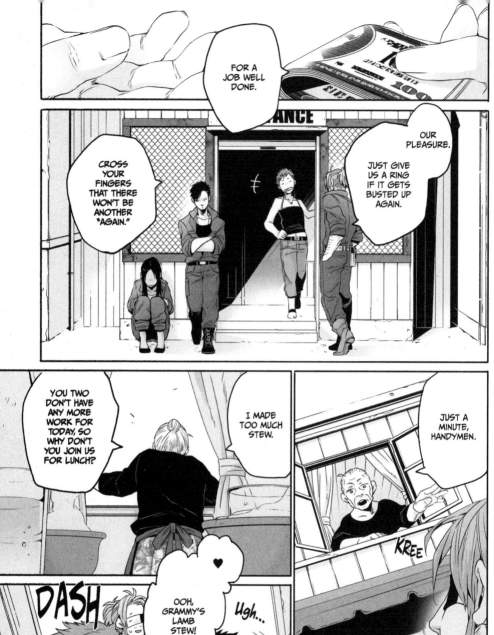
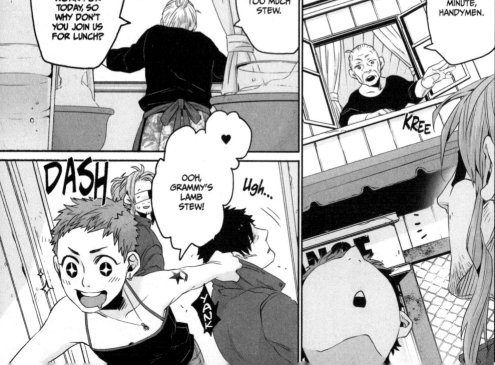

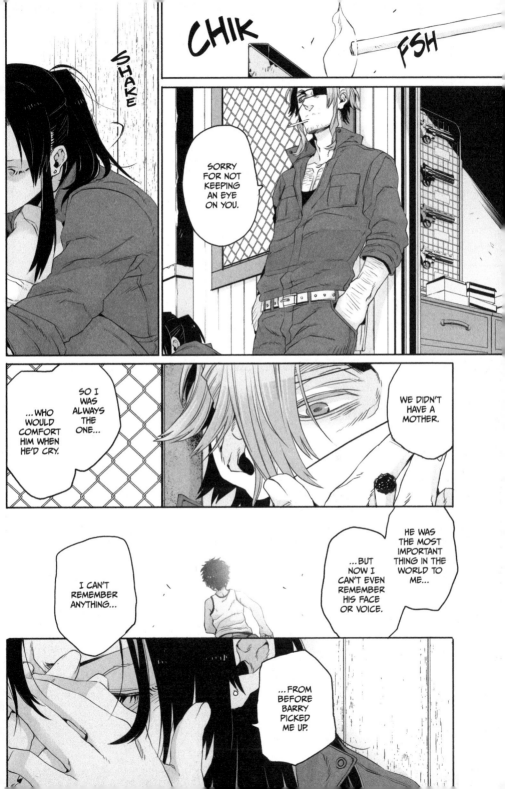

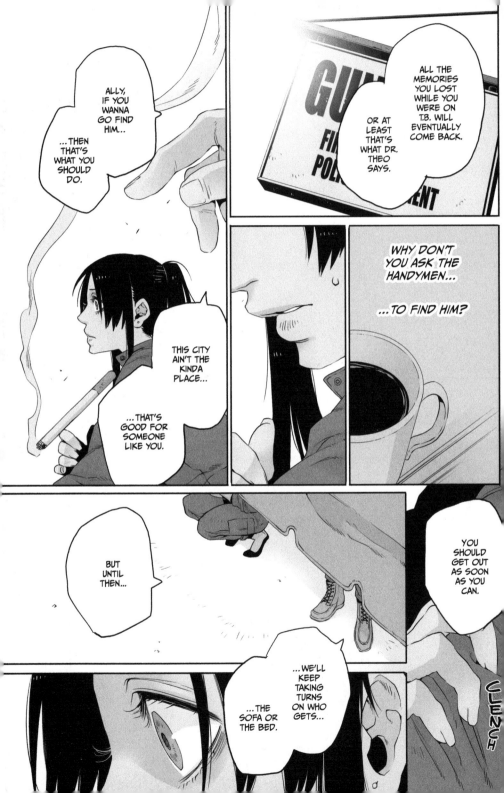

BUT FIRST THINGS FIRST. IT'S TIME TO EAT! ♥

ALLY!

HEY, ALLY, GET UP HERE!

BEFORE IT GETS COLD!

#17 END

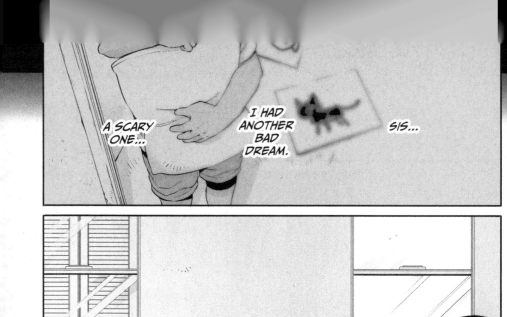

SIS...

I HAD ANOTHER BAD DREAM.

A SCARY ONE...

#18

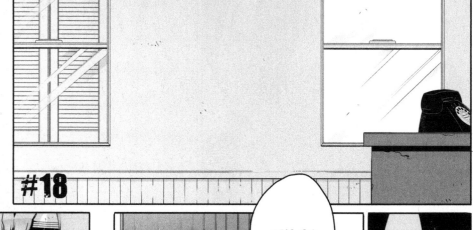

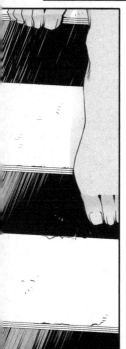

IT'S SO QUIET...

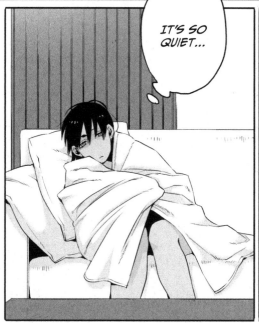

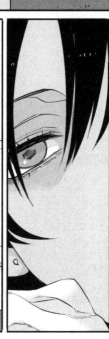

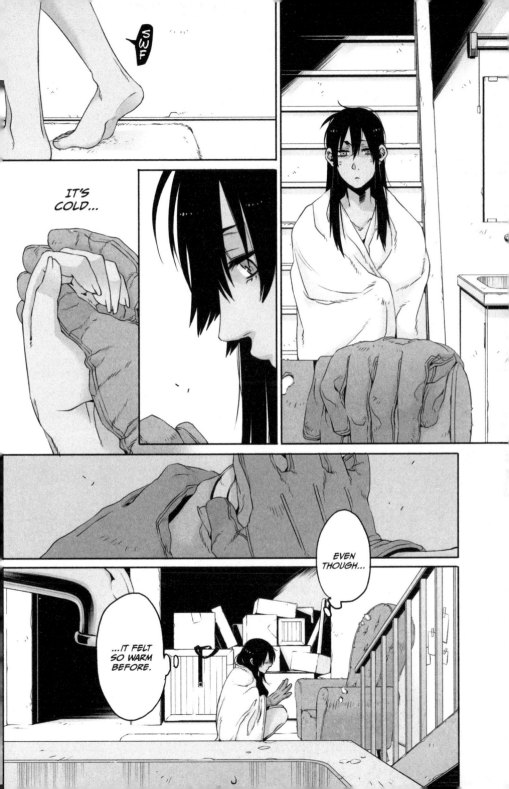

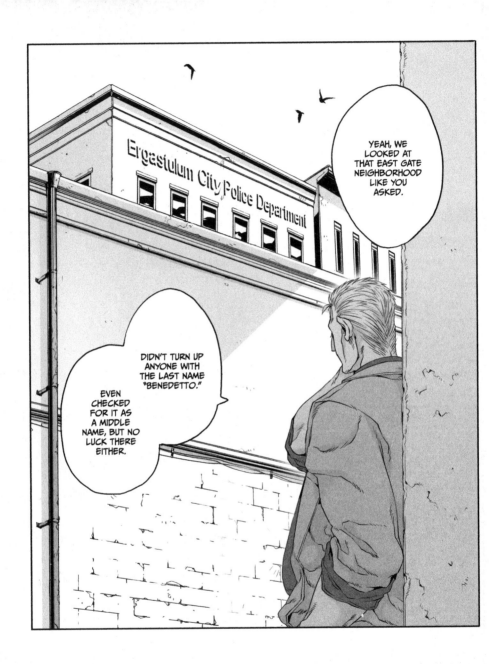

#18

WORICK, YOU GOTTA UNDERSTAND...

...THE POPULATION IN THAT AREA HAS A REALLY HIGH TRANSIENT RATE.

AND YOU DIDN'T FIND ANYONE WHO'D HEARD OF "ALEX BENEDETTO"?

EVEN IF HER LITTLE BROTHER'S STILL ALIVE...

...CHANCES ARE HE'S MOVED ON.

AND IF HE DID, IT'S GONNA BE HARD TO FIND HIM.

NOT A ONE.

LOOK, I MAY HAVE INS AS A COP, BUT THIS IS ERGASTULUM WE'RE TALKIN' ABOUT HERE.

GOVERNMENT CONTROL OF THE POPULATION RECORDS IS AT PARANOIA LEVELS.

AND THERE'RE NO LEADS FOR US TO FIGURE OUT WHERE THE FAMILY WAS FROM ORIGINALLY.

FROM THE DESCRIPTION YOU GAVE ME, THEY'RE MIXED RACE BLACK, ASIAN, AND WHO KNOWS WHAT ELSE.

THE OTHER THING IS THAT THEY MAY NOT'VE BEEN FROM THERE ANYWAY.

WHAT ABOUT A FAMILY REGISTER?

YEAH, I GET IT...

36

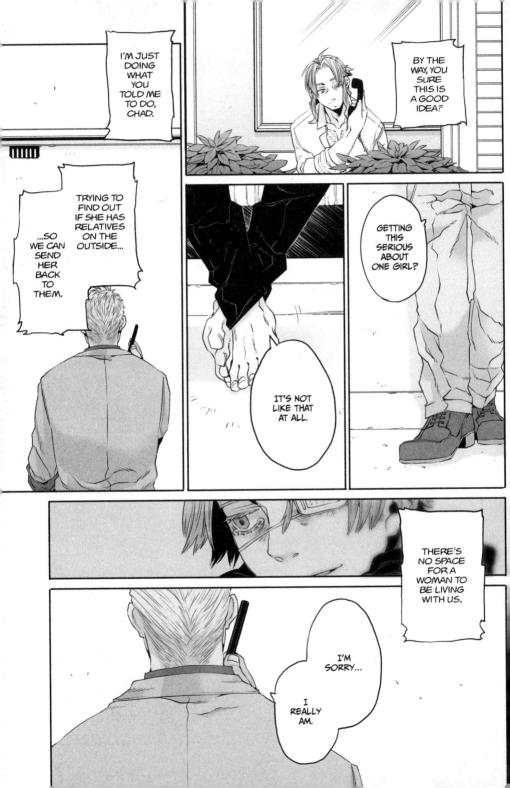

SO... LONG AS I'M AT IT, WANT ME TO LOOK FOR YOUR MOTHER?

VROOM

BEEP BEEP

ARE YOU SERIOUS? YOU REALLY THINK I'D WANT TO...

...TRACK DOWN MY HOOKER MOM AT THIS POINT IN MY LIFE?

SKREE

CHAD!

WE GOT A CALL IN ABOUT ANOTHER DEAD TAG.

NO... IT'S WORSE.

SAME THING AS BEFORE?

LOOKS LIKE IT'S FINALLY COMING DOWN...

WELL, SHIT.

ACCORDING TO THE WITNESSES, THE GUY WAS ATTACKED BY A GANG OF NORMALS.

IT WAS STRAIGHT-UP MOB VIOLENCE...

HOW AWFUL!

AND JUST WHEN WE'D BEEN FREE FROM IT FOR A WHILE...

IS THIS ANOTHER ONE OF THE HACKER MURDERS?

I HEARD IT WAS AN ANTI-TWILIGHT GROUP.

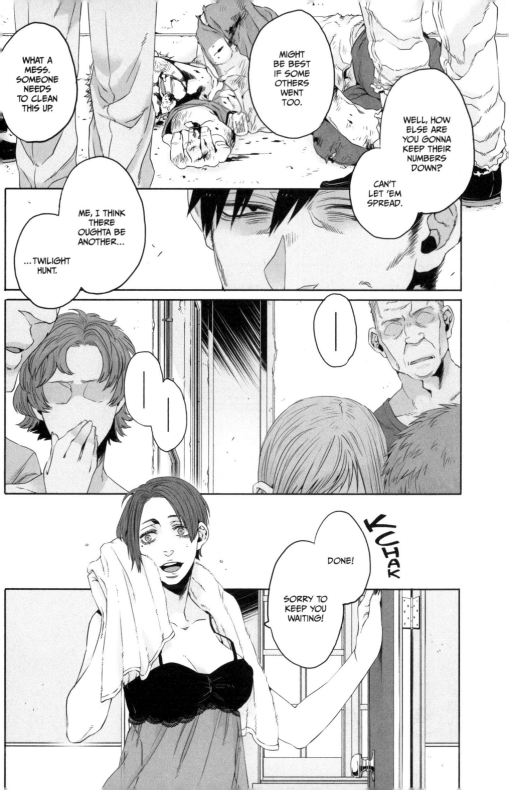

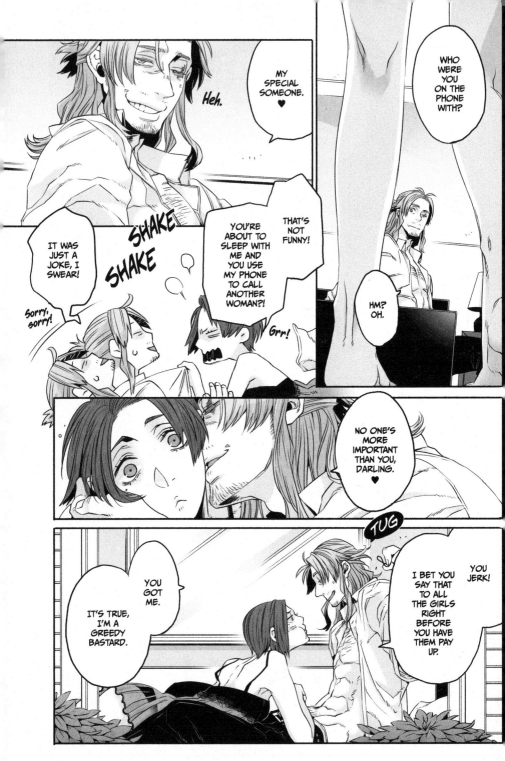

41

CREAK

...THAT PHONE BILL WITH YOUR BODY.

YOU'RE GOING TO PAY FOR...

YES, MA'AM! ♥

OH, RIGHT!

THERE'S ONE MORE THING...

?

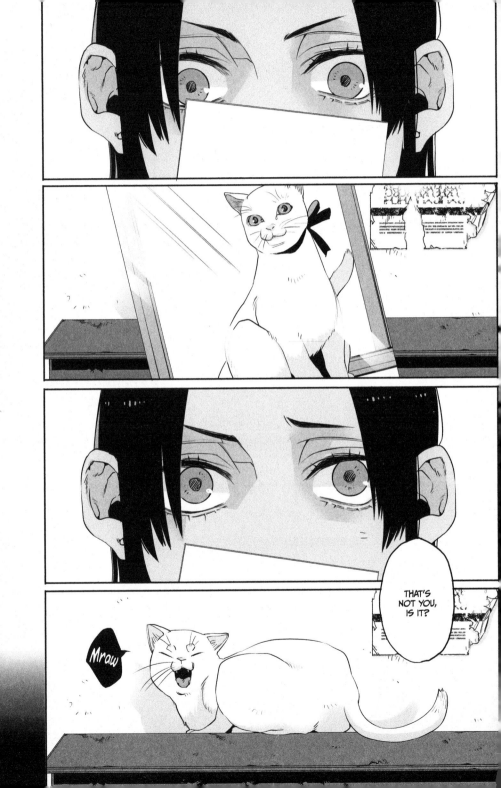

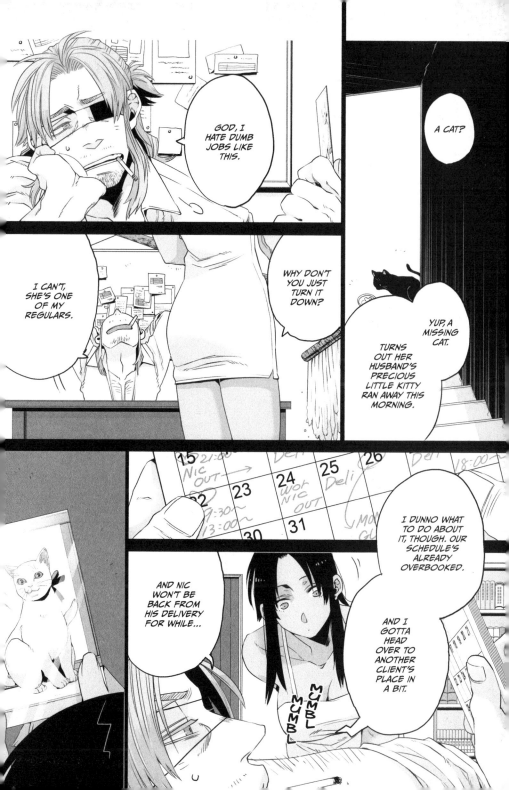

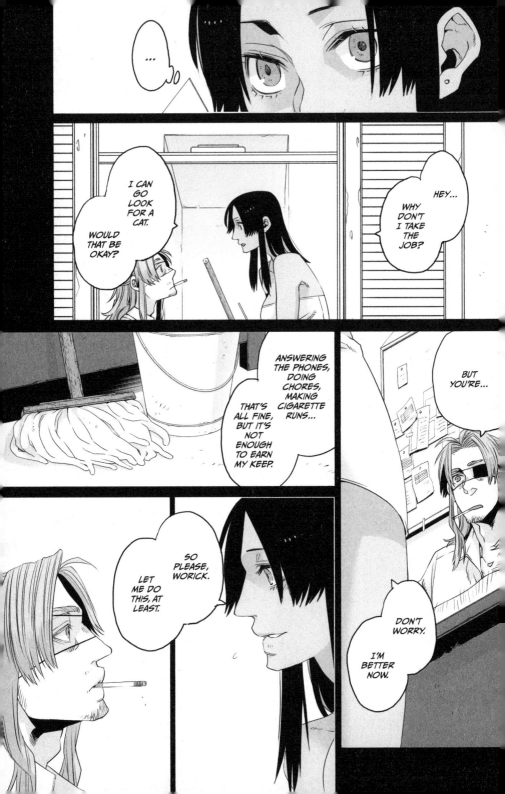

I'LL TELL NIC TO FIND YOU ONCE HE'S FINISHED.

Good luck.

THANKS!

FWIP

...

JUST DON'T GET INTO TROUBLE.

EASIER SAID THAN DONE.

THIS JOB MIGHT BE HARDER THAN...

...in this town.

There are a lot of cats...

...I THOUGHT IT WOULD BE.

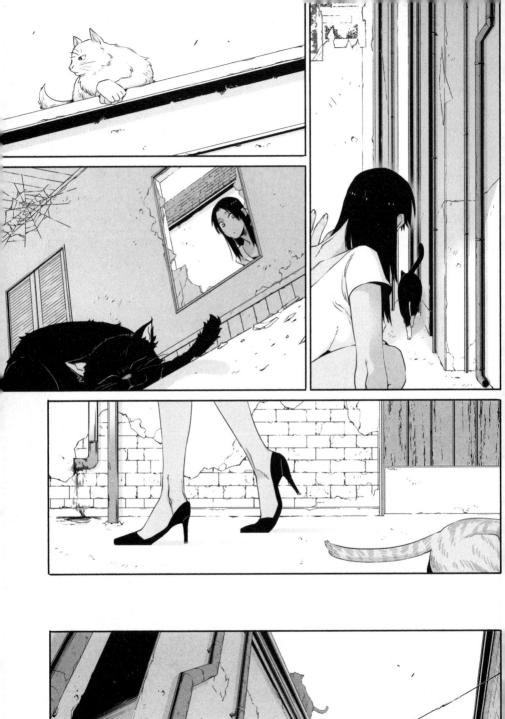

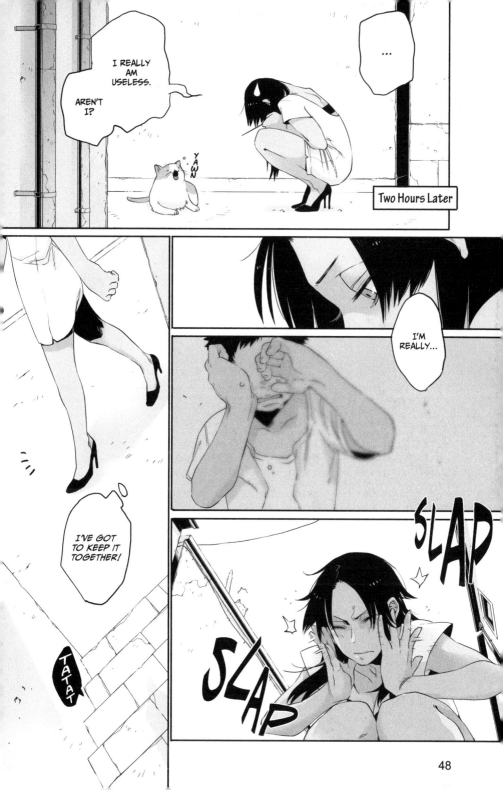

48

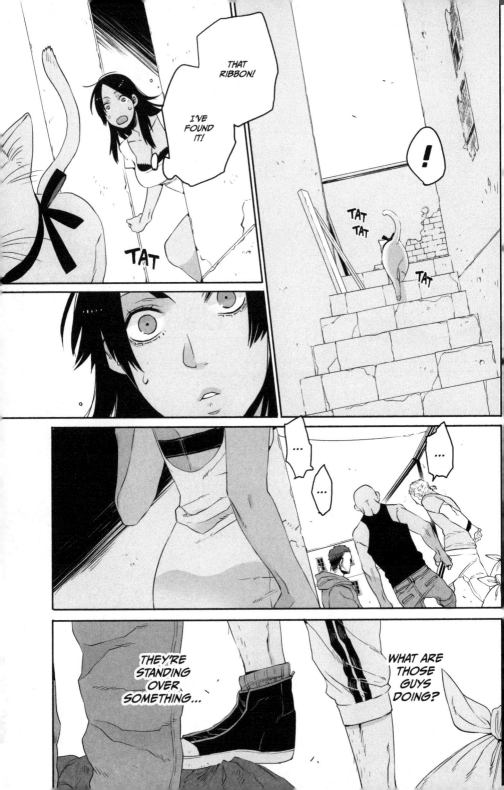

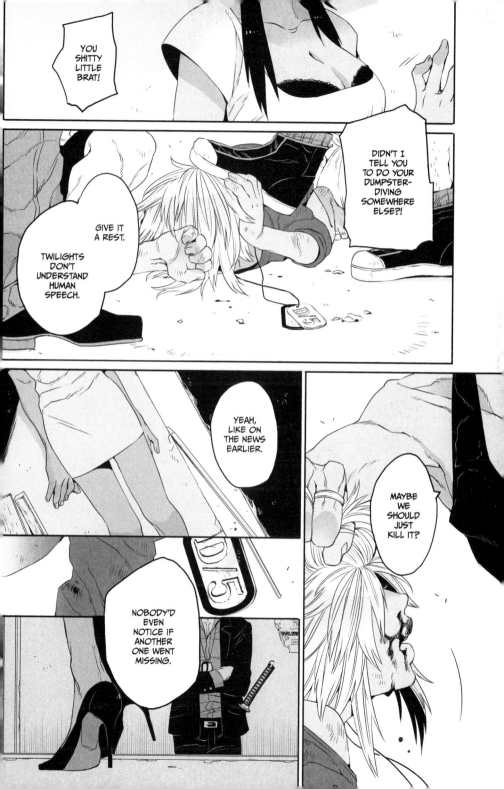

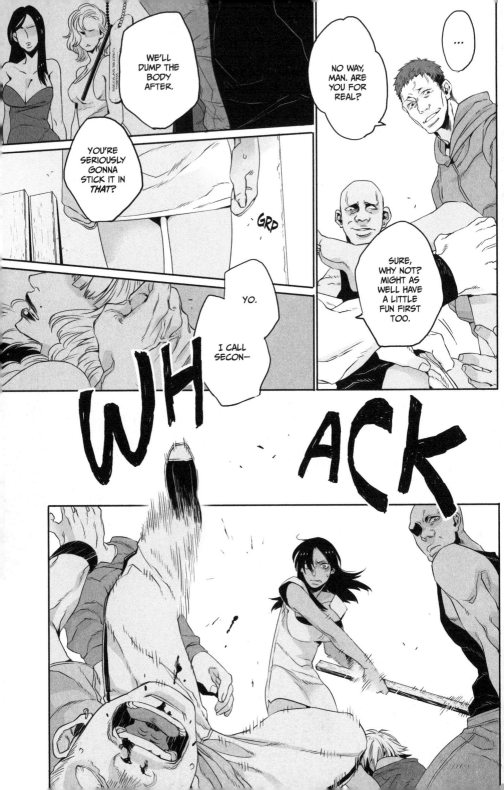

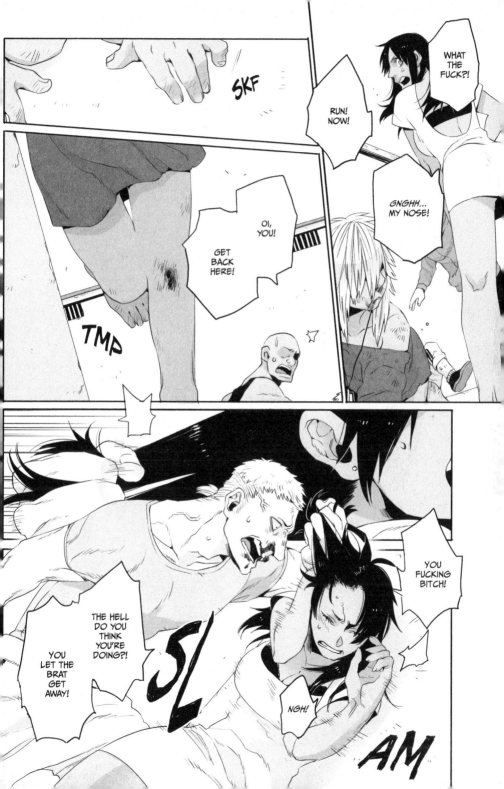

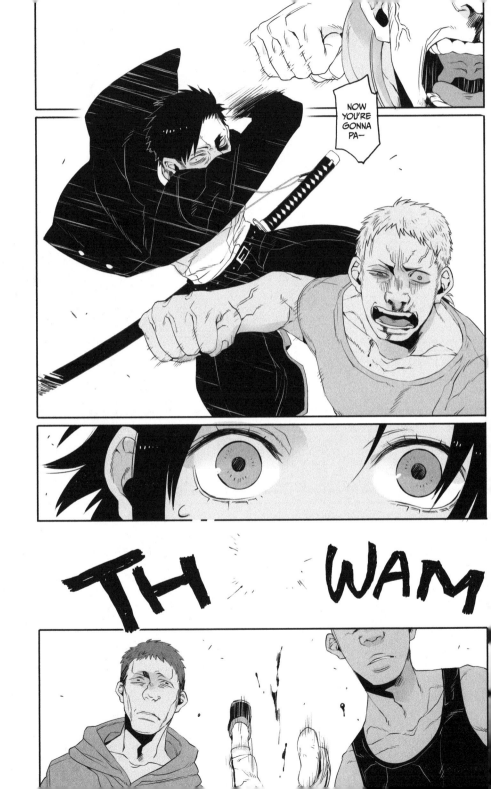

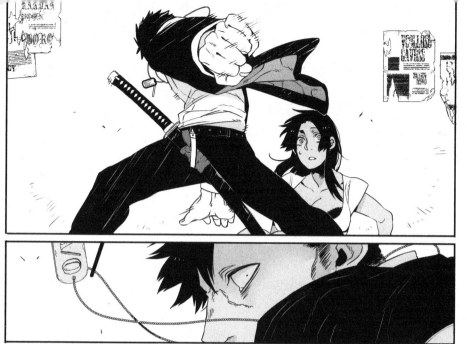

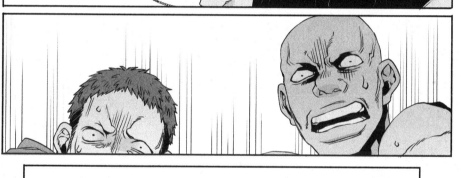

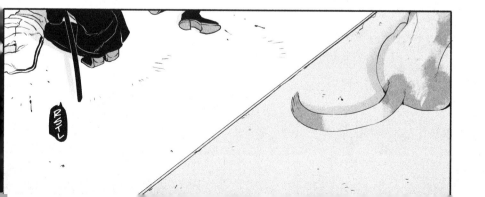

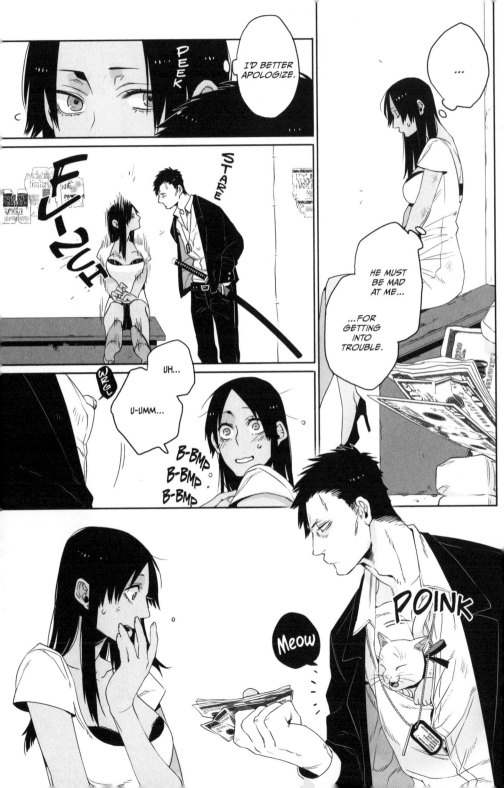

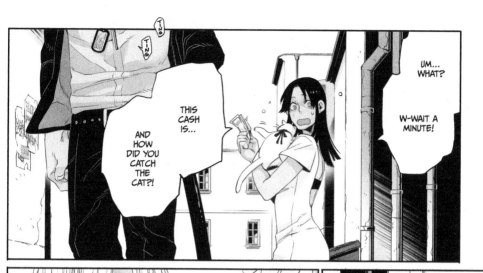

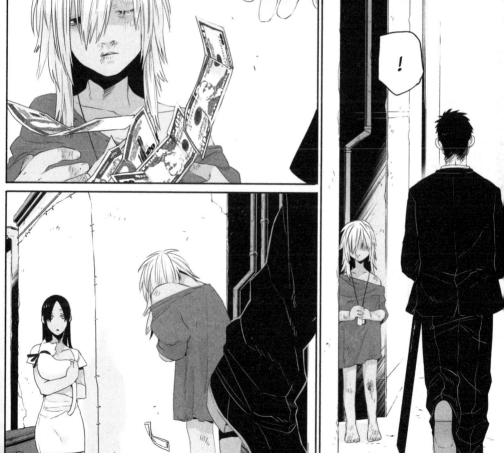

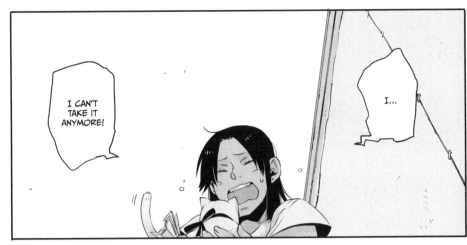

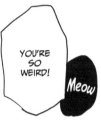

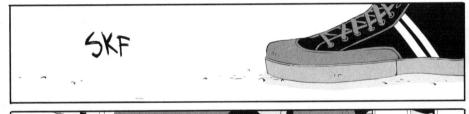

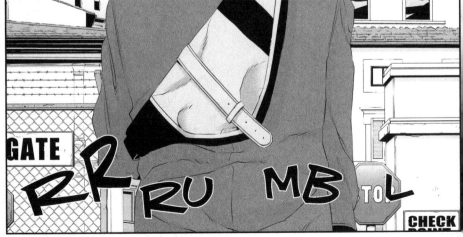

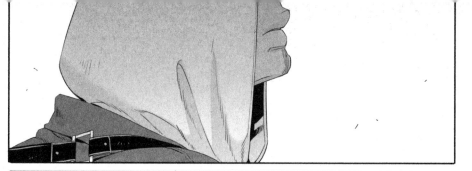

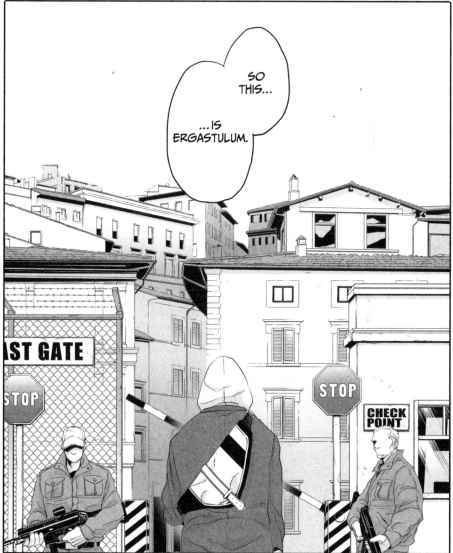

#18 END

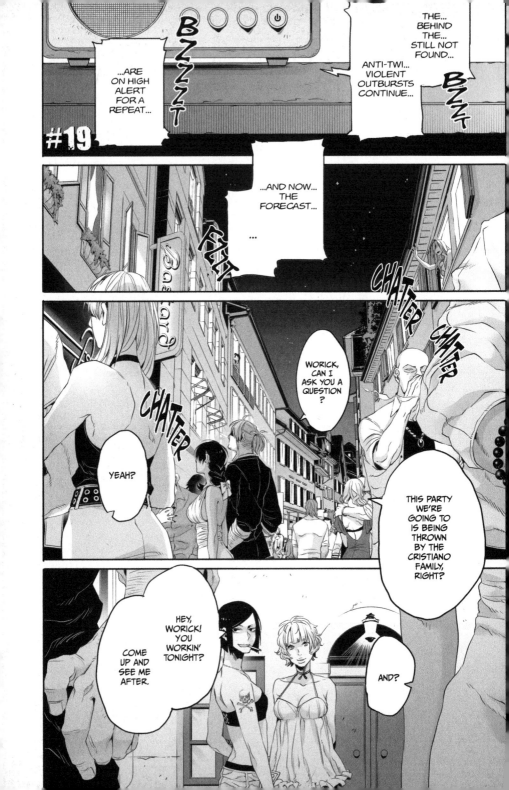

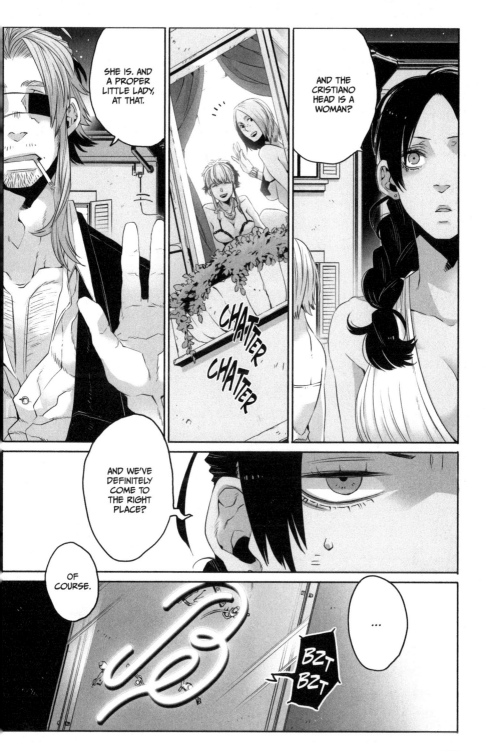

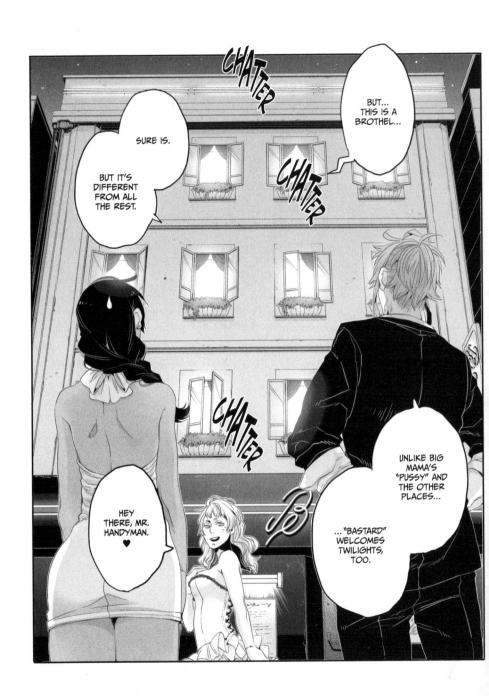

#19

YOU'RE LATE, WORICK ARCANGELO!

YOU'VE GOT A LOT OF NERVE MAKING ME WAIT!

WHAT TOOK YOU SO LONG?!

YO, HANDYMAN!

WELCOME TO BASTARD.

FW

UF!

THESE, FOR YOU.

MY SINCERE APOLOGIES, MISS CRISTIANO. I HAD TO STOP AND PICK SOMETHING UP.

...FINE. YOU'RE FORGIVEN.

SNAP

HERE'S YOUR ENTRY WRISTBAND. DON'T TAKE IT OFF.

MAYBE SHE'S THE BOSS'S DAUGHTER?

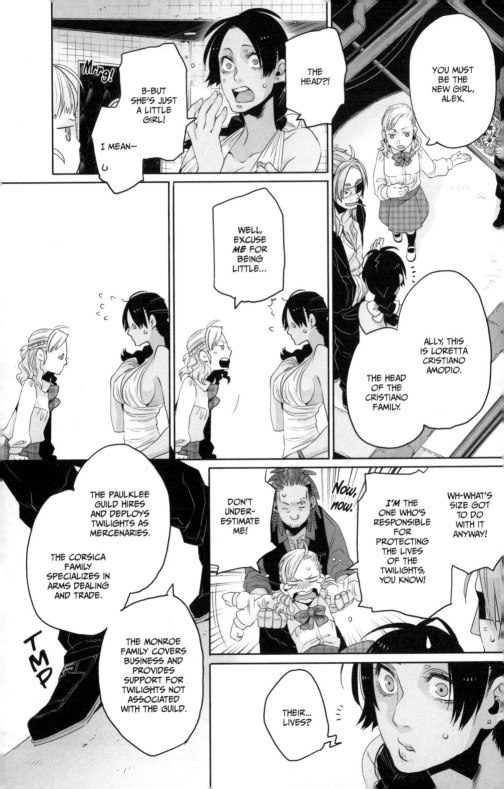

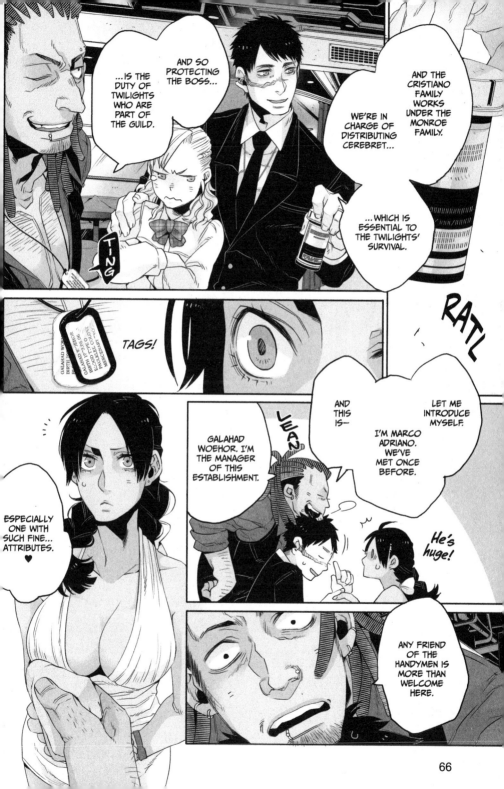

66

SLAP

HEY, GAL...

WHAK

GALLY, YOU LECH!

YOU PERV!

MISSY, THAT'S NOT VERY LADYLIKE— OUCH! OW!

I'M SORRY! I'M SORRY!

WHAK

GLINT

THAT'LL BE $100 A PEEP.

Huff!

Hiff!

Hah!

Hah!

TMP TMP

TMP

IF YOU WANT A WOMAN, THERE'RE PLENTY OF WHOREHOUSES AROUND!

I TOLD YOU I DON'T RUN THAT KINDA PLACE! SCRAM!

...

...

PLEASE WAIT! THAT'S NOT WHAT I—

...

NOW, GIT! GET OUTTA HERE!

TMP

68

SNIFF

THERE'S MORE THAN USUAL.

THIS COULD GET UGLY FAST.

SEVEN ON THE STREET, FIVE IN THE ALLEY, AND MORE TO THE NORTH.

WSH WSH

FOR HOW LITTLE MONEY THEY'RE PAYING US, YOU'D THINK THEY COULD HIRE ON MORE PEOPLE.

...

LOOKS LIKE THE ANTI-TWILIGHTS HAVEN'T LEARNED THEIR LESSON YET.

YEP.

Hrmph!

NEITHER HAVE YOU.

NO KIDDING. BUT THE CRISTIANO FAMILY ALWAYS HAS BEEN AND ALWAYS WILL BE A SMALL, WEAK ORGANIZATION.

THAT'S WHY THEY'LL NEVER BE ABLE TO COME OUT FROM UNDER MONROE.

DROP IT.

HE ASKED IF WE COULD COVER TODAY'S ESCORT RUN BY OURSELVES.

HE'S PROBABLY SHORT ON STAFF.

ISN'T GAL COMING?

BZZT

FLARE

THE FUNNY
THING IS...

...IT'S
THANKS TO
THEIR BAD
LUCK...

...THAT WE'RE
LUCKY ENOUGH
TO MAKE SOME
STEADY CASH.

HEY,
PARTNER!

DON'T
KILL ANY
NORMALS.

FLARE

OKAY...

HERE
THEY
COME.

OH, FOR
SHIT'S SAKE!
WHY CAN'T
YOU JUST
SUCK IT UP
AND LIP-
READ...

ALL WE'RE
HIRED
TO DO IS
ESCORT
THE
TWILIGHTS
TO—

HUH?

WS

SH

...UNTIL
I'M DONE
TALKING!

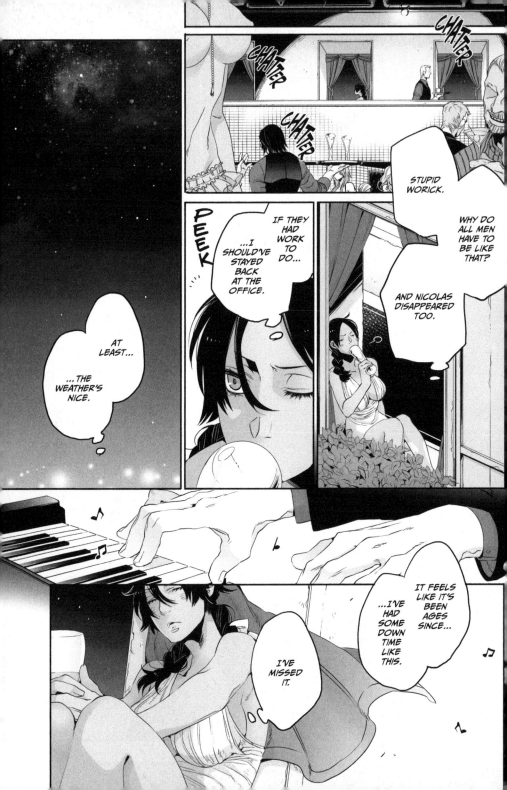

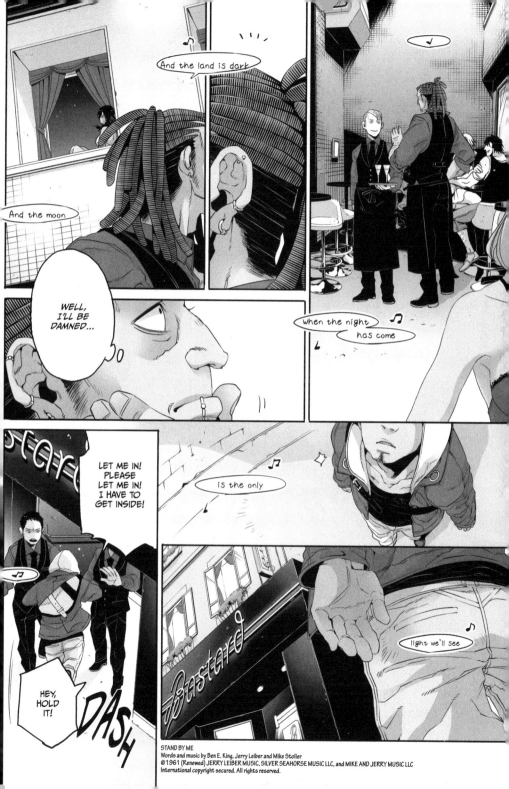

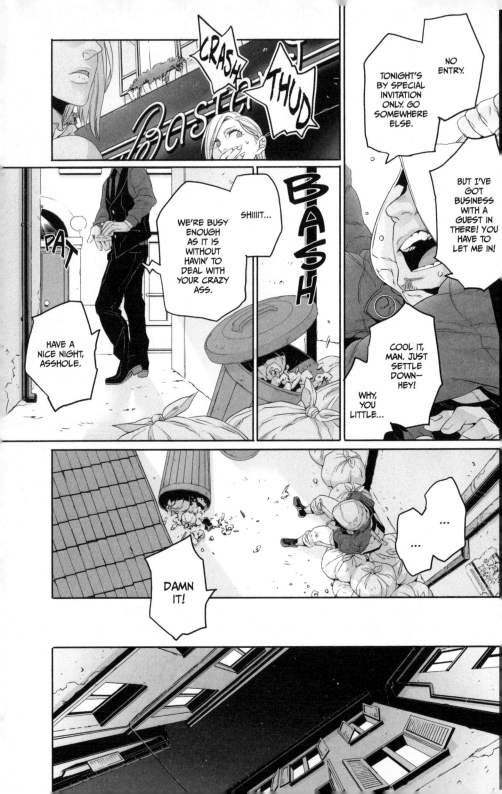

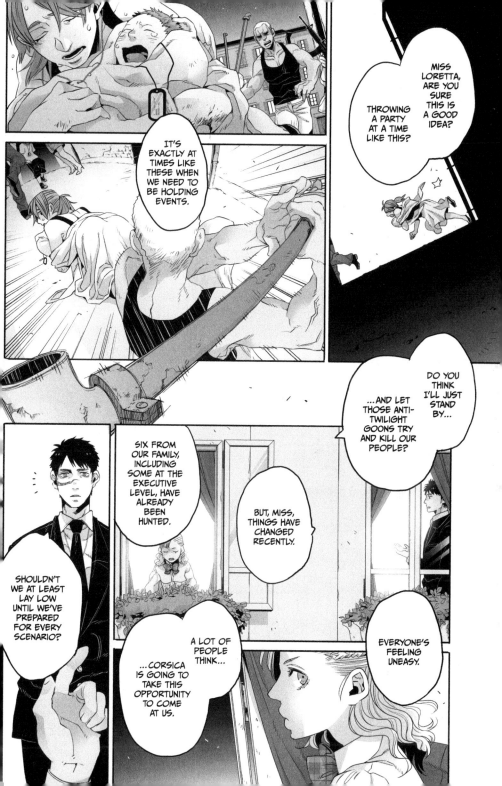

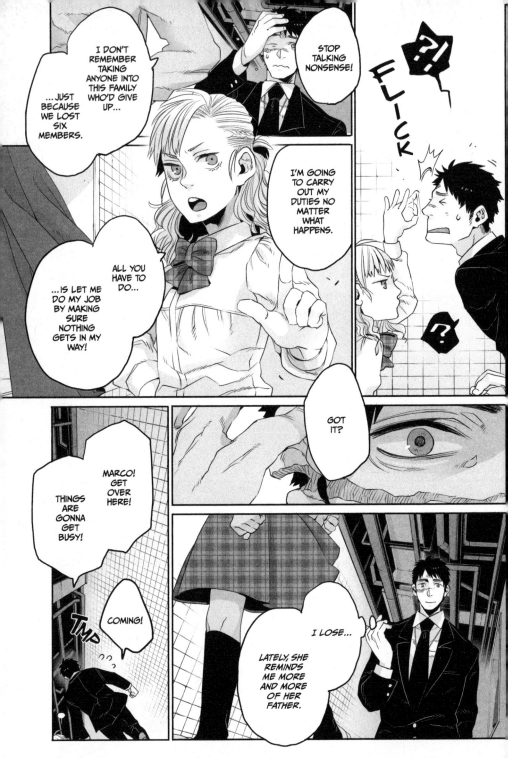

75

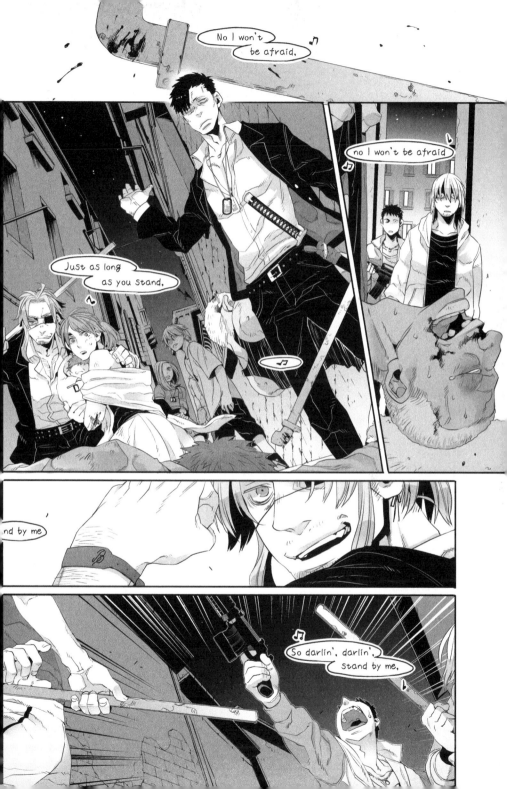

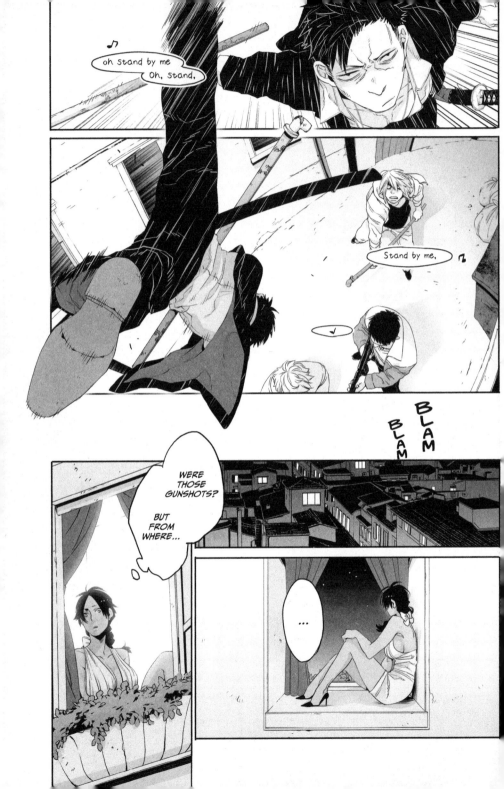

I HAVE TO GET HELP!

MISS CRISTIANO—

SEE THAT BUILDING THERE...

...ACROSS THE WAY?

MMPH!

BLAM
BLAM
BLAM
BLAM

!

BUT—

I NEED YOU TO ACT LIKE YOU DON'T KNOW THEM, EITHER.

WE'RE BEING WATCHED. MOVING CEREBRET ISN'T THE ONLY THING WE'RE DOING THAT THE LAW DOESN'T LIKE.

LEGALLY, THE CRISTIANO FAMILY DOESN'T HAVE THE RIGHTS TO DEAL WITH TWILIGHTS AT ALL.

IF WE BETRAY ANY EVIDENCE THAT THE MISSY IS DIRECTLY INVOLVED, THINGS'LL END BADLY FOR EVERYONE.

SO WE CAN'T GO OUT THERE AND HELP THE HANDYMEN. I'M SORRY.

OH...

TING

AS YOU CAN SEE, THIS JOINT'S FULL UP WITH REFUGEES.

IT TAKES UP A LOTTA MY TIME.

...CAN GET INVOLVED WITHOUT CAUSING PROBLEMS FOR THE MISSY.

ON THE OTHER HAND, HIRED MUSCLE LIKE ME, SOMEONE WHO'S NOT OFFICIALLY PART OF THE FAMILY...

I ACTUALLY HAVE TO BE CAREFUL THAT WE DON'T GET TOO MUCH BUSINESS.

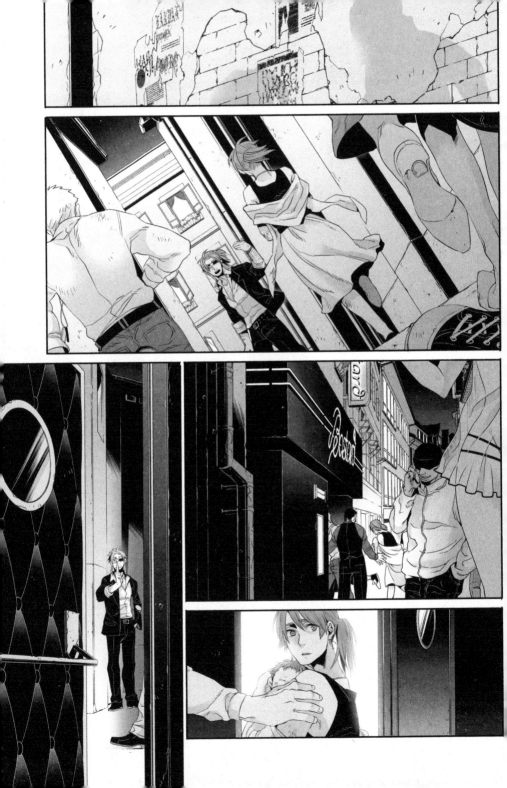

THANK YOU.

THANK YOU SO MUCH!

THANK YOU FOR COMING.

PLEASE LEAVE THE REST TO US AND JUST RELAX.

THE REASON PEOPLE ARE SO SCARED OF TWILIGHTS IS BECAUSE THEY DON'T KNOW THEM.

I THINK...

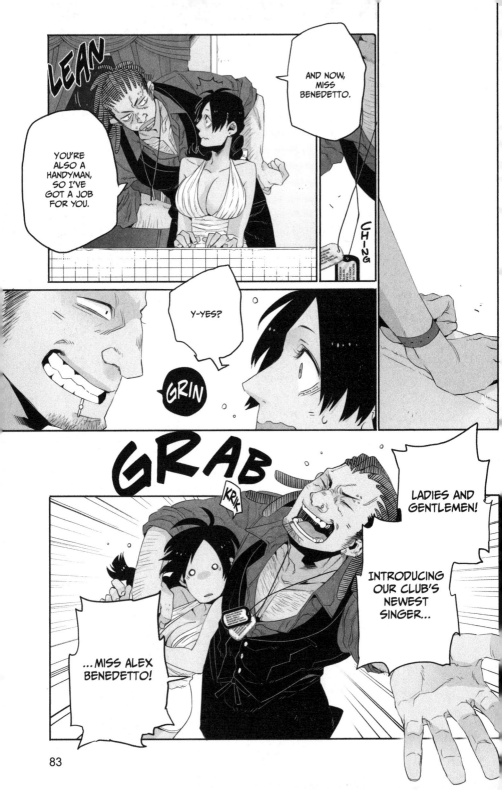

83

W-WAIT A SECOND! THERE'S NO WAY I CAN SING IN PUBLIC!

WH-WHAAAT?!

CLAP

Woo-hoo!

SHE'S A GAL FROM THE MUSICAL TOWN OF EAST GATE!

LET'S GIVE HER A WARM WELCOME!

CLAP

CLAP

CLAP

GOOD.

WHAT ARE YOU TALKING ABOUT? ISN'T THAT WHY YOU'RE HERE? WORICK SAID SO.

OUR PREVIOUS SINGER QUIT ON US.

YO, ALLY. YOU LIKE MY SURPRISE GIFT?

BZZT

SLIP

HUH? YEAH, SHE'S HERE. I'LL PUT HER ON.

GLOOM

HE HEARD ME?!

HE TOLD ME YOUR VOICE IS OUT OF THIS WORLD.

84

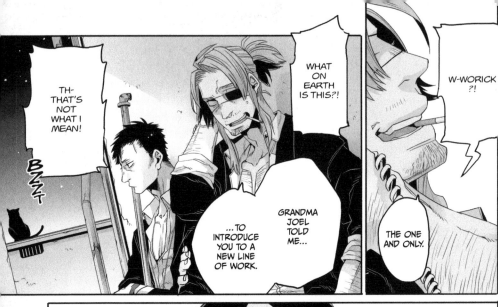

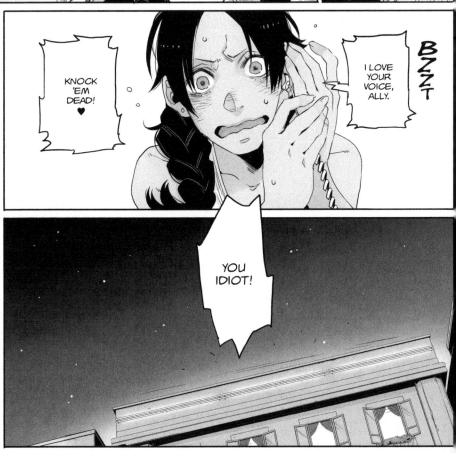

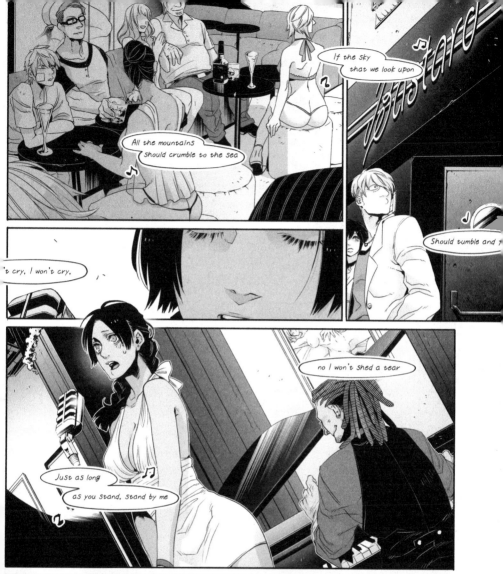
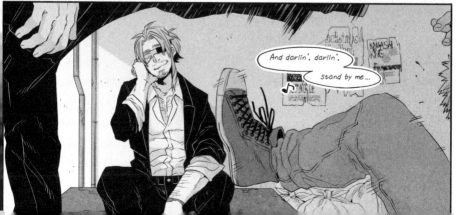

ERICAAA...

TOLD YOU SO. THEY'RE ALL USELESS.

COME OOOON...

LET'S GO ALREADY.

I'M BORED.

I'M HUNGRY...

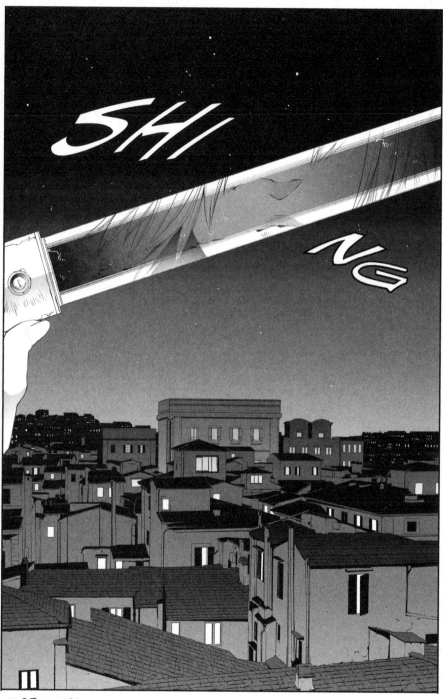

#19 END

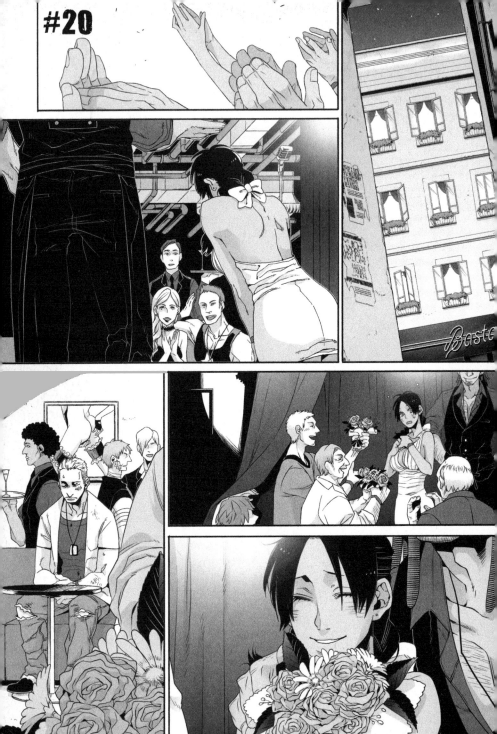

THOSE ANTI-TWILIGHT FACTIONS AREN'T TOO SMART, ARE THEY?

THE REASON WHY WE HAVEN'T BEEN ABLE TO EXTERMINATE YOU VERMIN...

...IS BECAUSE THERE'S THIS NICE LITTLE GIRL WHO KEEPS FEEDING YOU.

THEY'VE BEEN TRYING SO HARD TO WIPE YOU OFF THE FACE OF THE EARTH...

...BUT THEY CAN'T UNDERSTAND WHY THEY KEEP FAILING.

SOB

SOB

SO IT'S TIME FOR US...

...TO HELP.

HIC

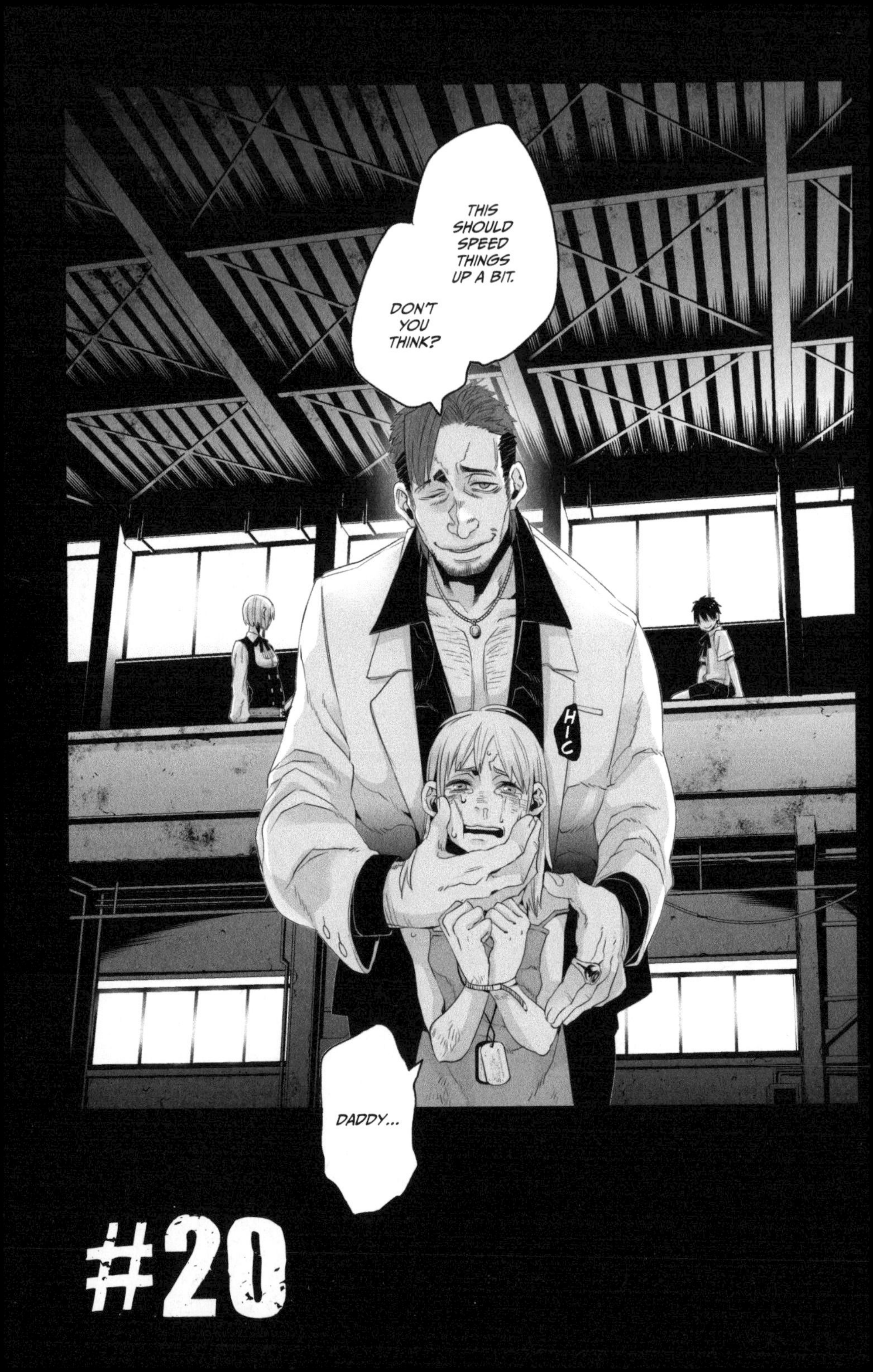
THIS SHOULD SPEED THINGS UP A BIT.
DON'T YOU THINK?
HIC
DADDY...
#20

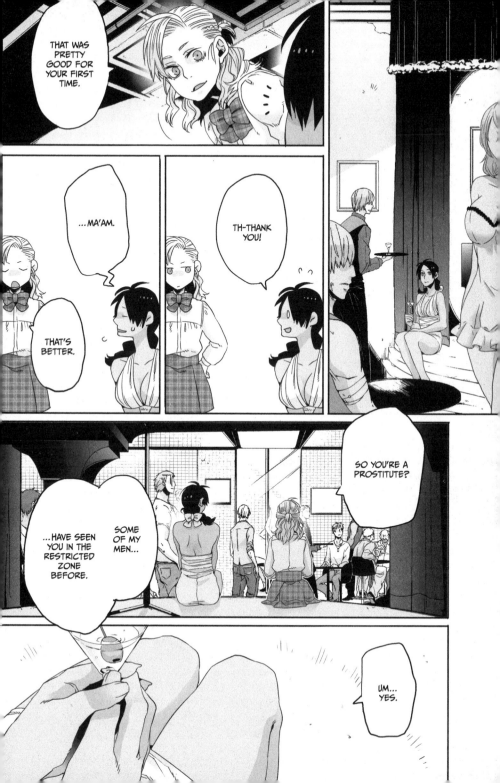

THAT REMINDS ME.

SINCE YOUR HEAD IS STILL ATTACHED TO YOUR NECK, YOU MUST BE PRETTY LUCKY. AND NOW YOU'VE GOT...

ONE OF OUR GIRLS JUST QUIT...

...SO THERE'S AN OPEN ROOM AVAILABLE.

...INSPECTOR ADKINS AND THE HANDYMEN LOOKING OUT FOR YOU.

....!

YOU'D...

...PROBABLY FIT IN WELL HERE.

MY MOTHER WAS ALSO...

...A PROSTITUTE.

I'M KIDDING.

EVERYONE TELLS ME WHAT AN AMAZING WOMAN SHE WAS.

BUT SHE DIED RIGHT AFTER GIVING BIRTH TO ME.

SEE? THAT'S HER IN THAT PICTURE.

SHE WAS THE FIRST SINGER HERE.

SHE WAS ON THE STREETS UNTIL MY DAD FELL IN LOVE WITH HER AT FIRST SIGHT AND MARRIED HER.

SHE'S, UM... BEAUTIFUL...

YOU HAVE A GUEST FROM THE MONROE FAMILY!

UNLIKE YOU...

...SHE COULDN'T HANDLE THE T.B. WITHDRAWAL.

BE RIGHT THERE.

MISS!

96

POP

HELLO, IVAN. IT'S BEEN A WHILE.

MISS CRISTIANO, I HAVE SOMETHING FOR YOU FROM THE MONROE FAMILY.

OOH! UNCLE DANNY'S BEING SO GENEROUS AGAIN!

KNOWING YOU HAVE ALL THOSE TWILIGHTS TO TAKE CARE OF, HE FIGURED YOU COULD USE THE FUNDS.

HE SAID, "TELL HER TO SPEND IT WISELY."

Hm?

WHAT'S THAT SMELL?

SNFF

I DON'T KNOW WHAT TO SAY...

I CAME STRAIGHT HERE AFTERWARDS.

AH. MY APOLOGIE

I HAD TO DEAL WITH A CORPSE REMOVAL.

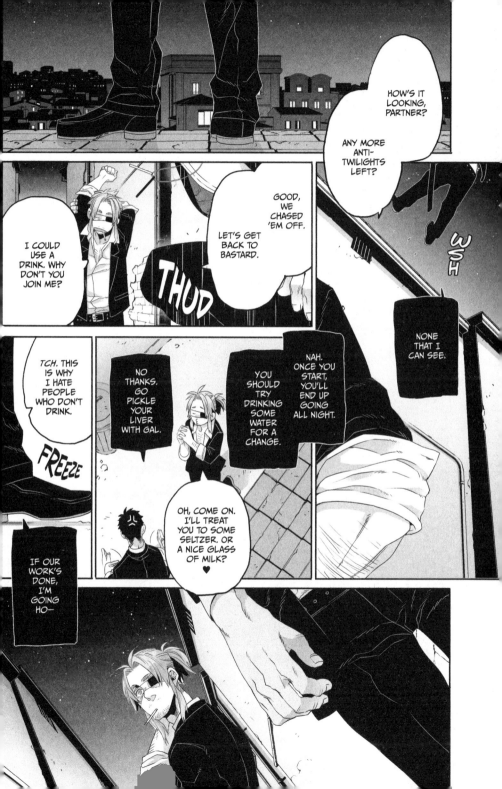

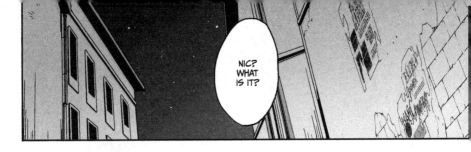

NIC?
WHAT
IS IT?

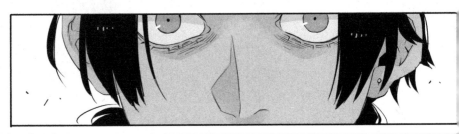

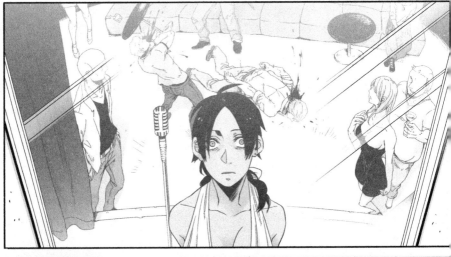

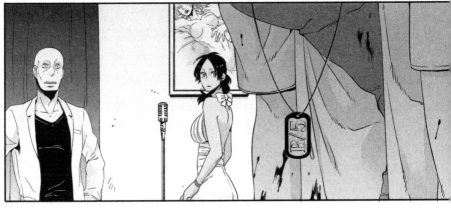

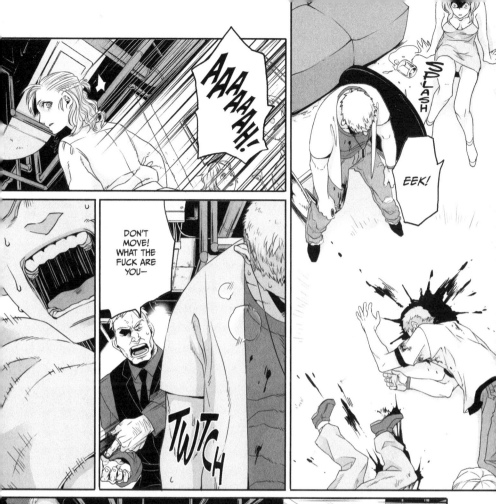

AAAAAAH!

SPLASH

EEK!

DON'T MOVE! WHAT THE FUCK ARE YOU—

TWITCH

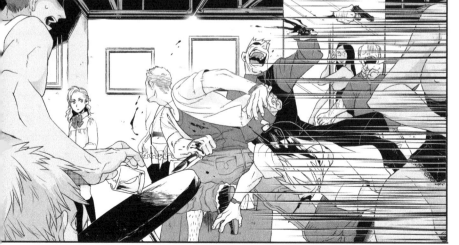

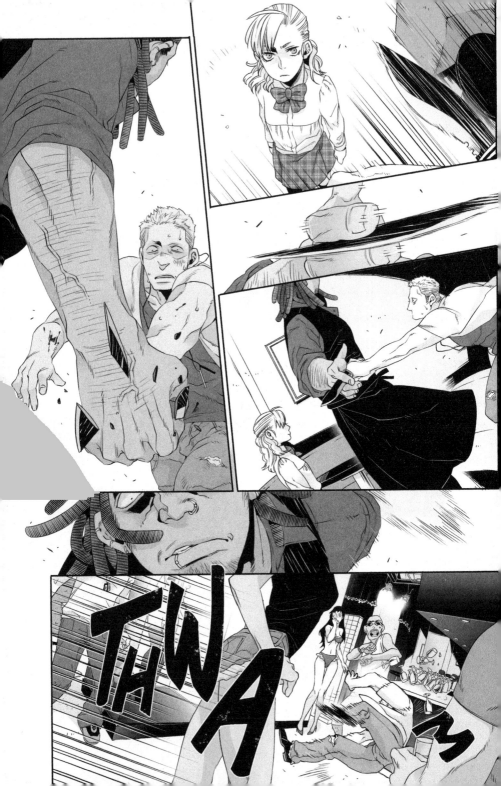

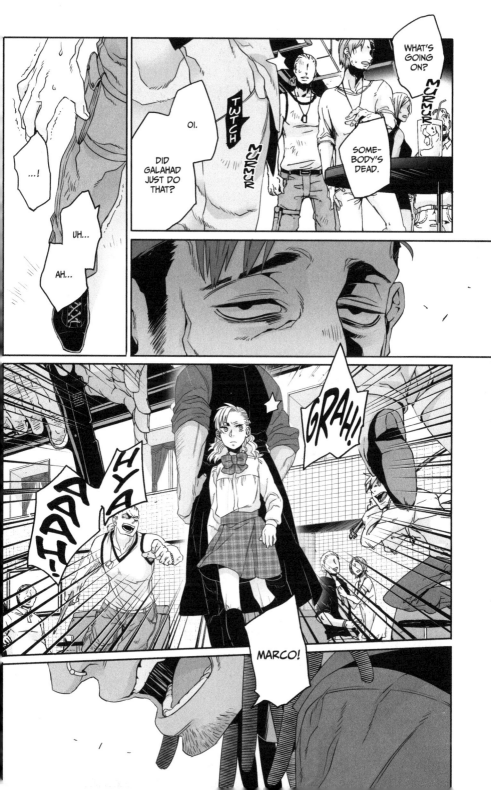

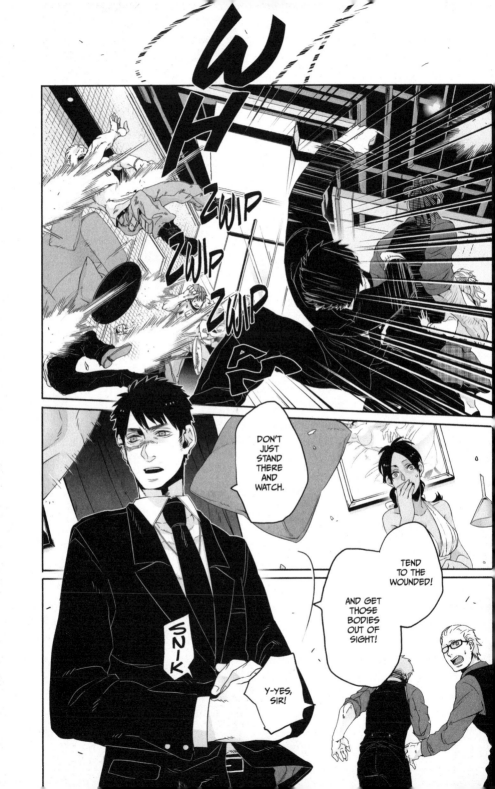

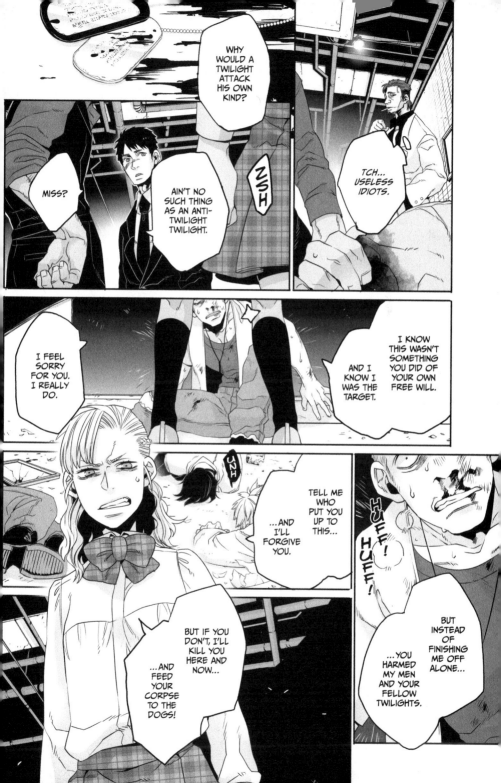

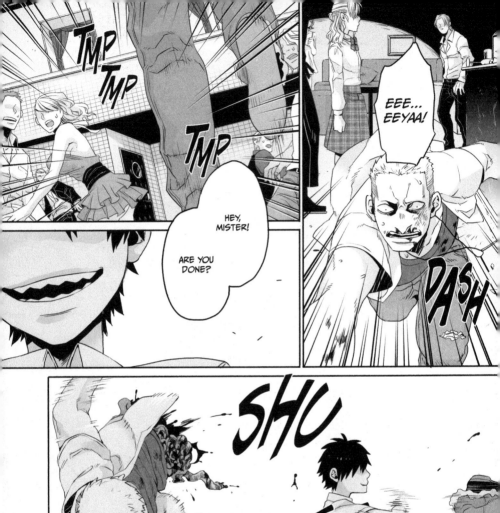

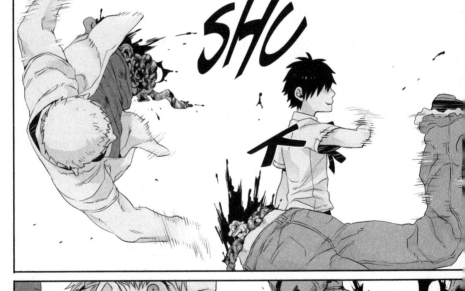

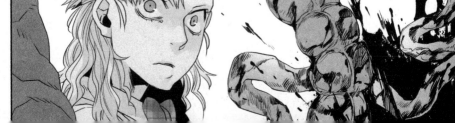

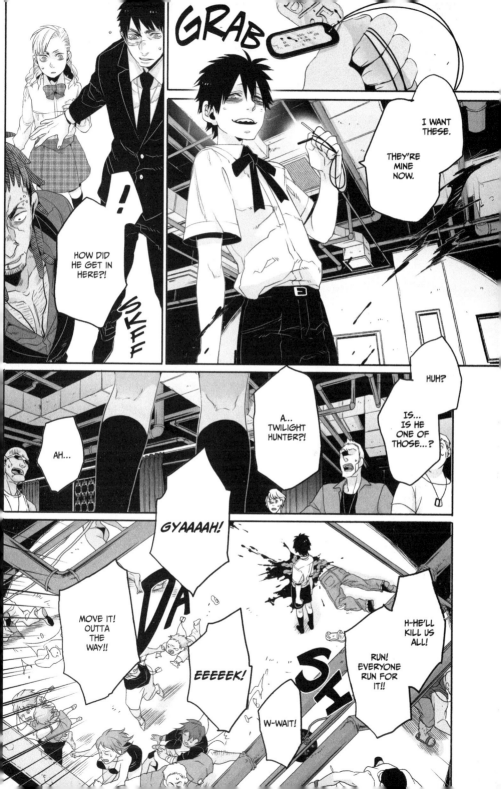

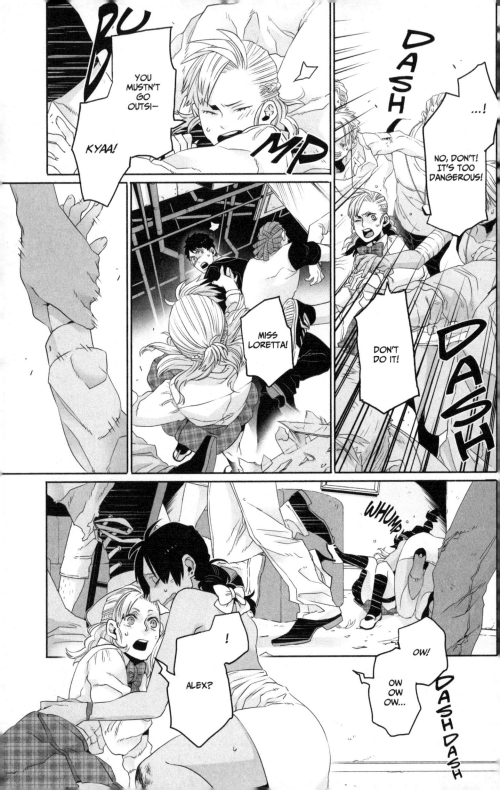

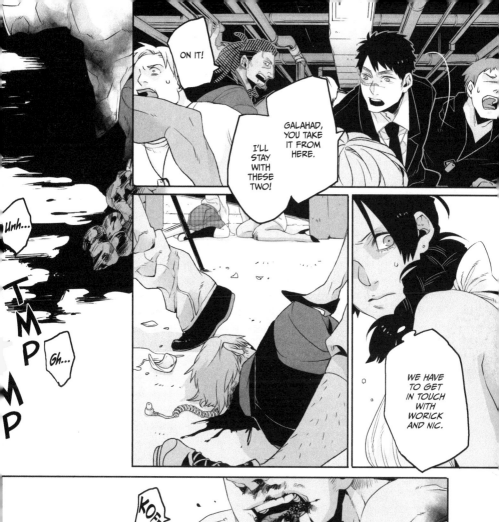

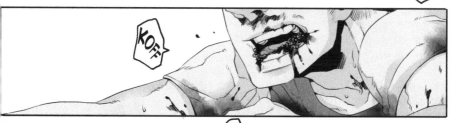

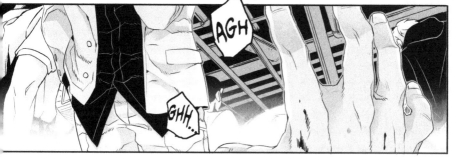

YOU PROBABLY WANT TO KNOW...

...ABOUT YOUR WIFE AND DAUGHTER.

WELL, WE TOOK CARE OF THEM... WE STRIPPED THEM DOWN, CHOPPED THEM UP, AND THREW THEM AWAY.

WHAT A MESS. YOU POOR MAN.

YOU SHOULD HAVE HEARD THEM CRY. IT WAS EXCEPTIONAL.

FSHT

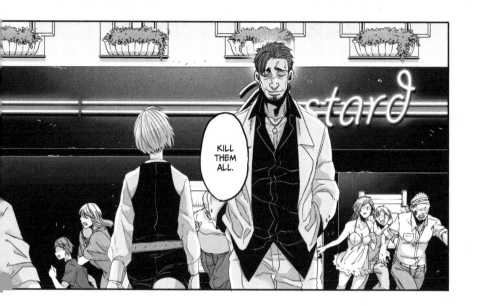

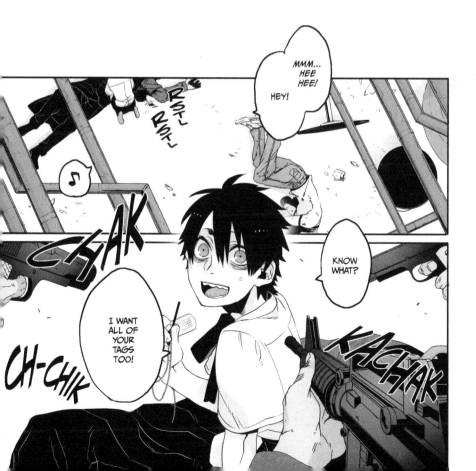

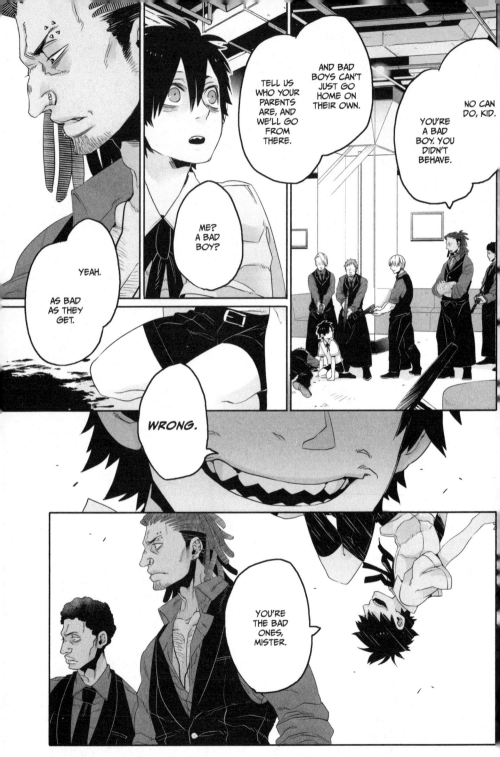

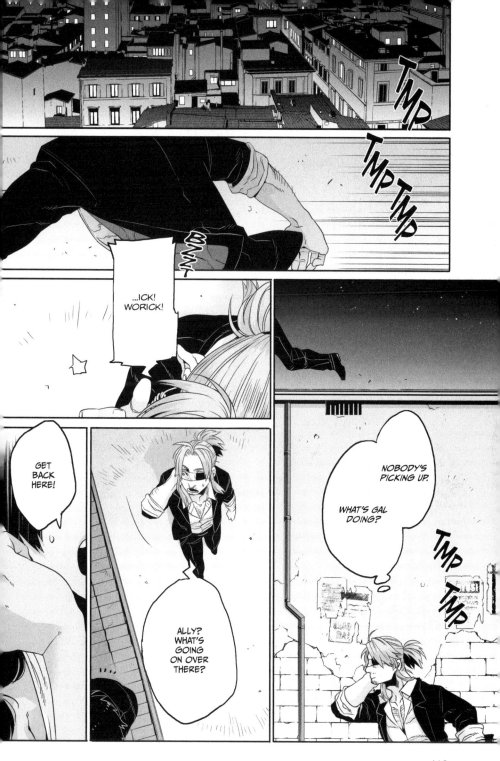

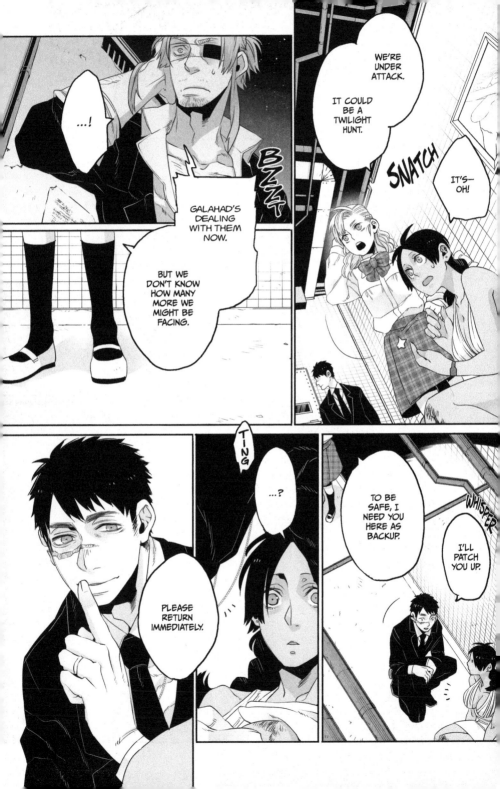

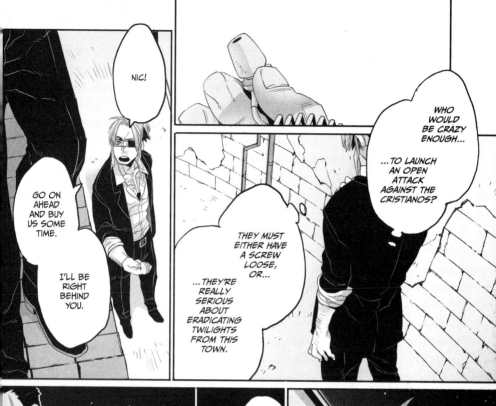

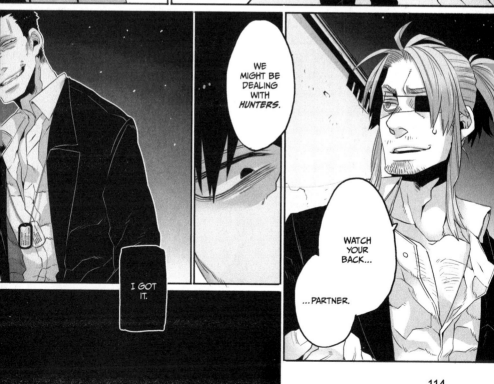

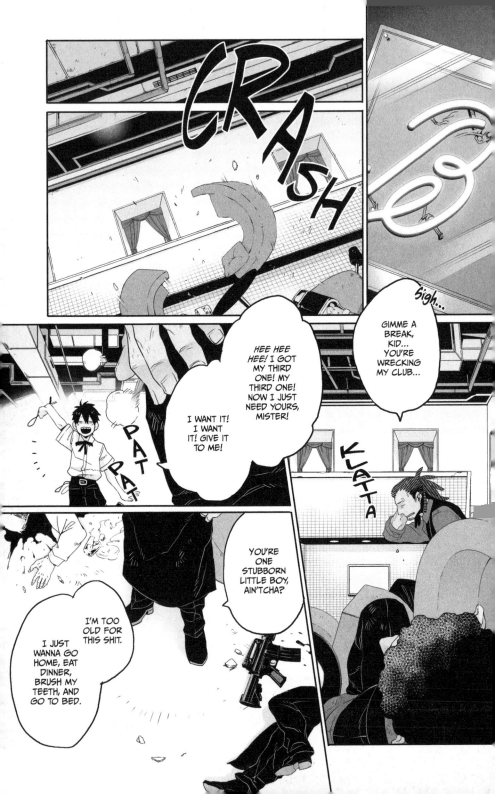

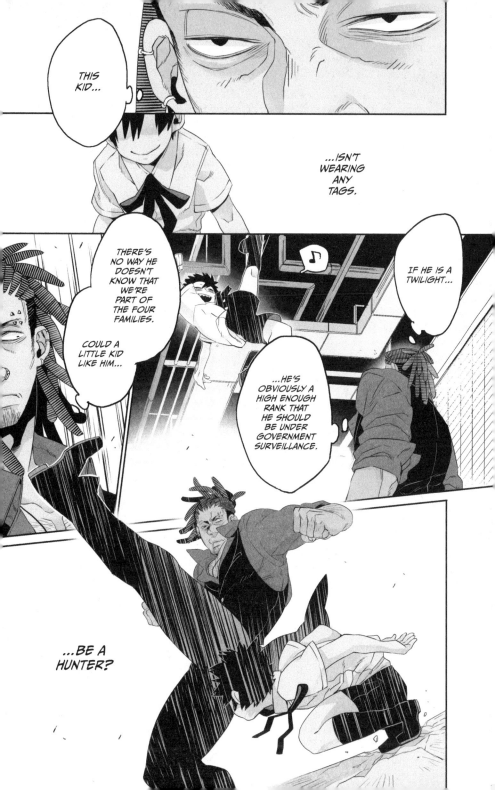

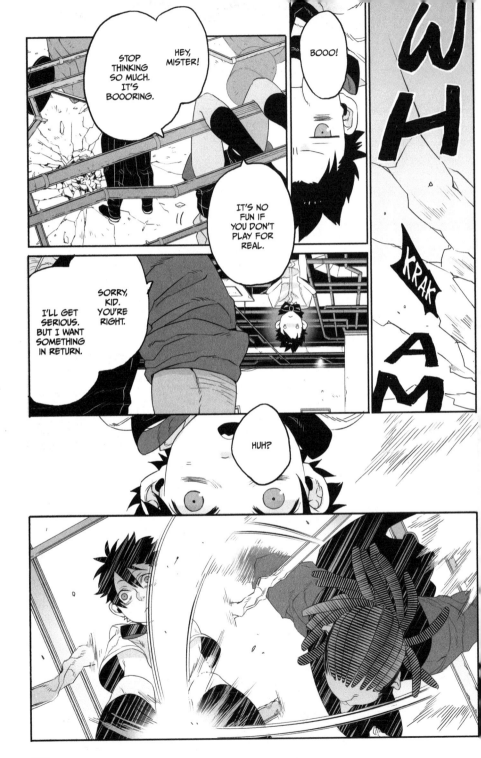

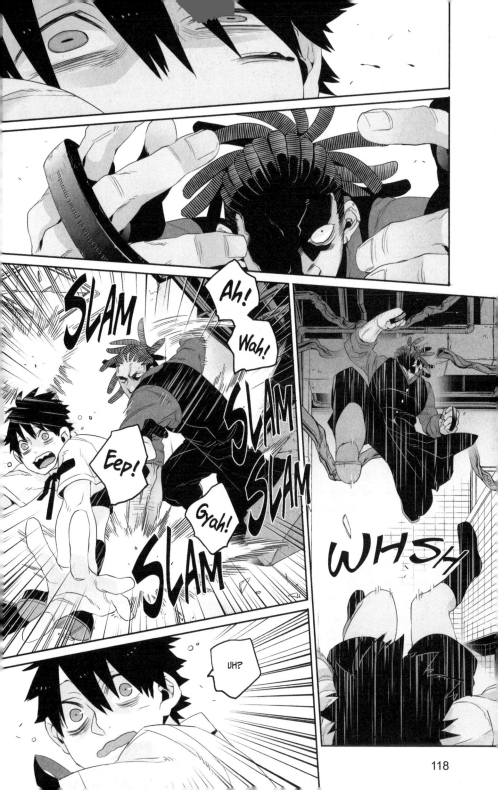

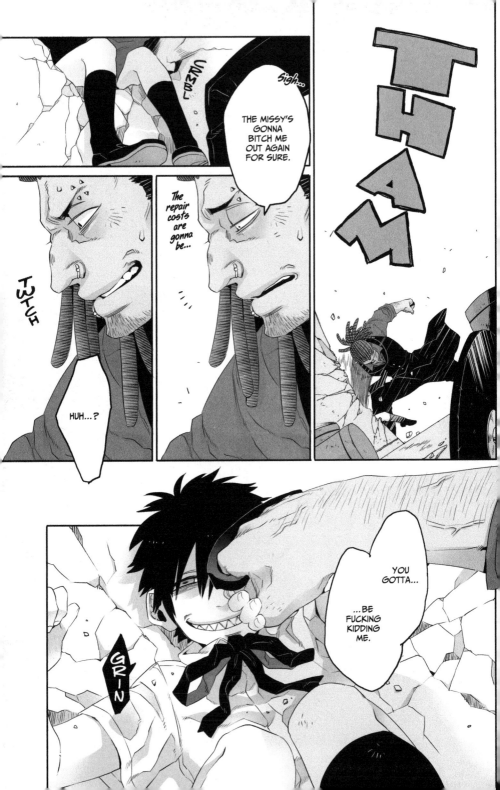

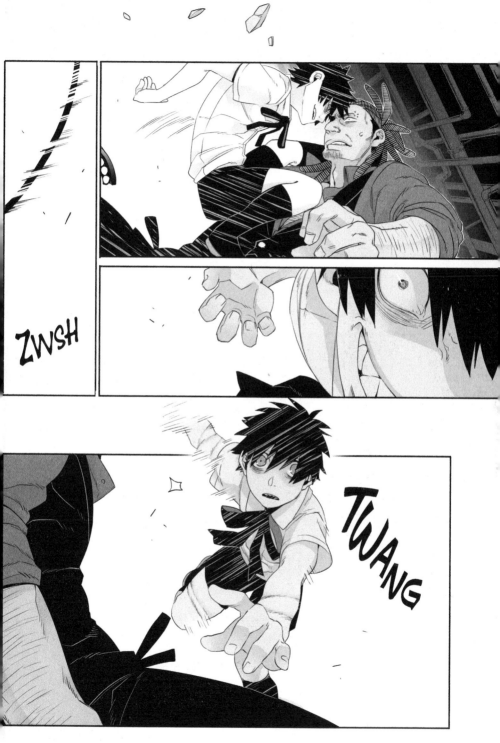

120

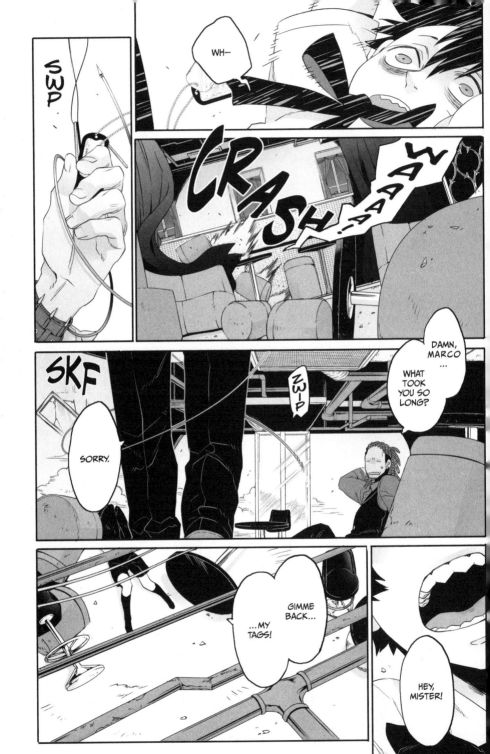

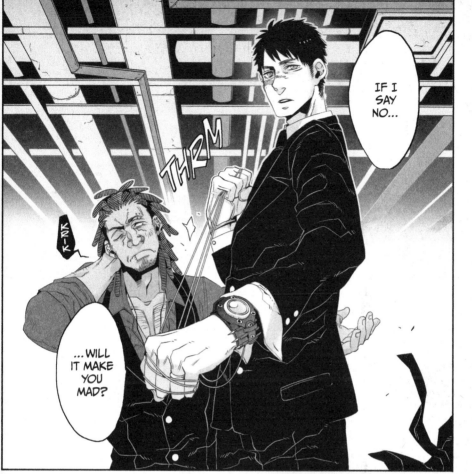
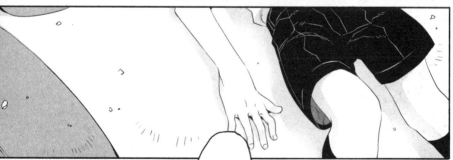

#20 END

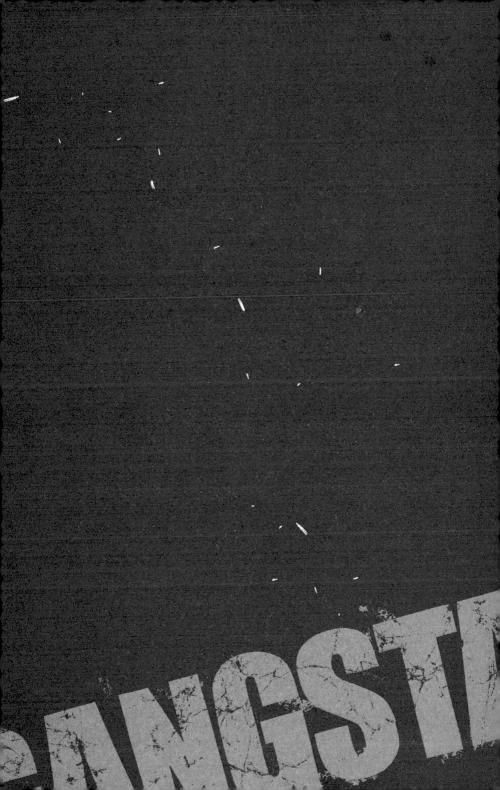

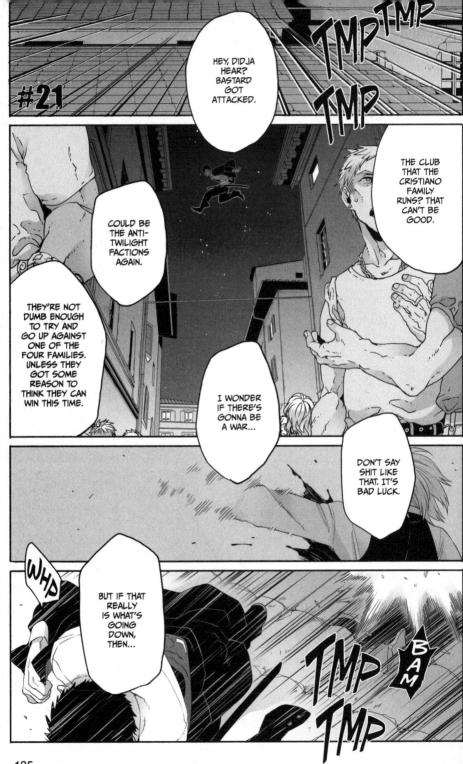

125

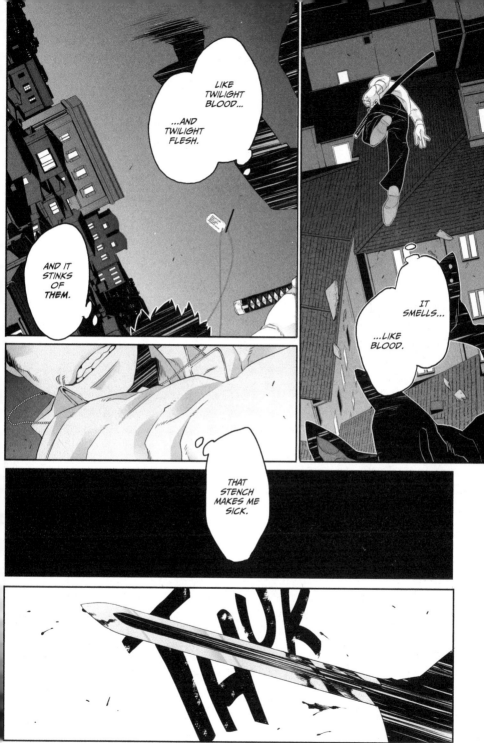

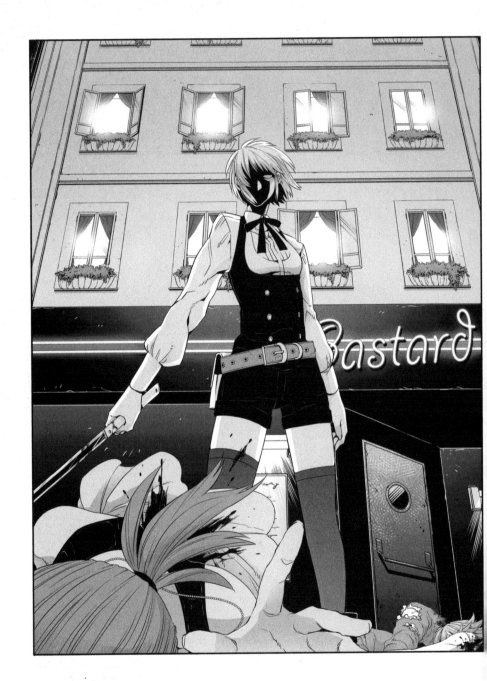

#21

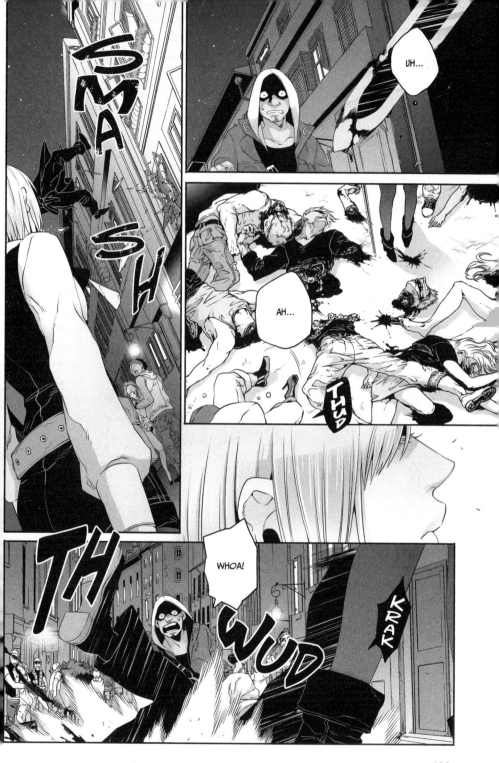

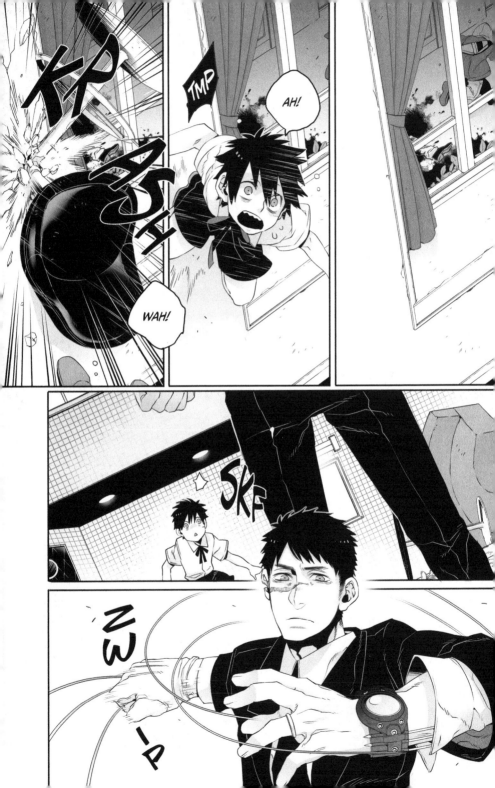

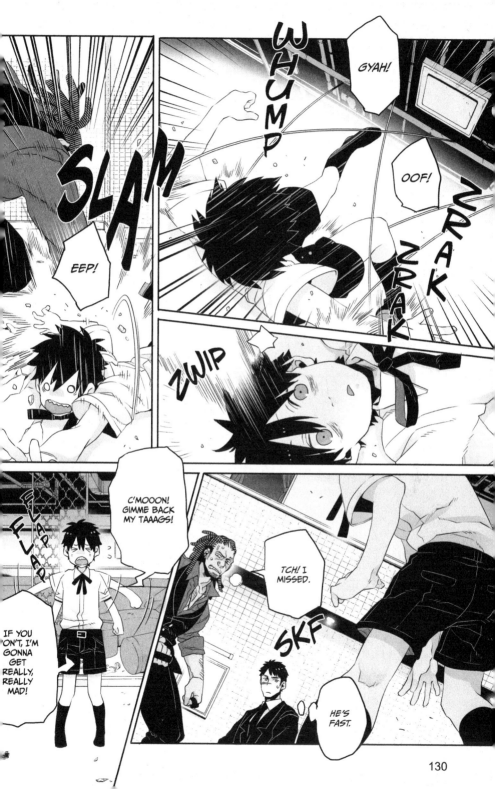

130

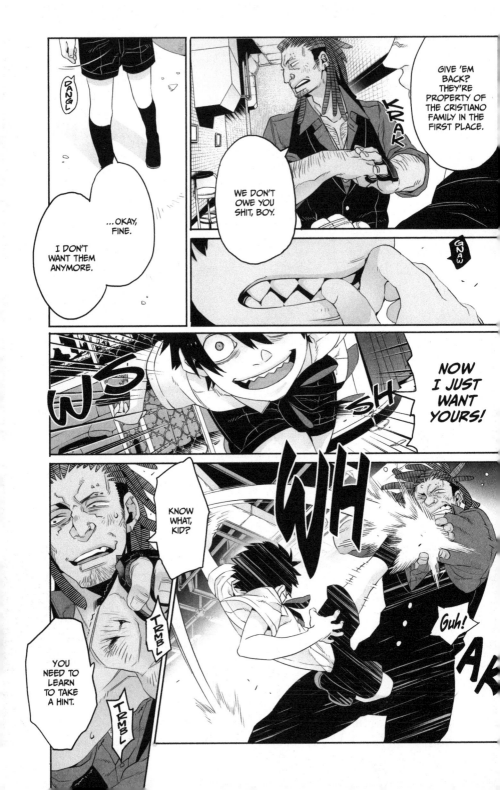

SKFF

KRA NG

KREE

KREE...

SLAM

BUT IN THE END...

MIGHT BE TOO MUCH TO HANDLE.

...HE'S STILL JUST A KID.

AND HE'S QUICK.

I KNEW IT. HE'S EITHER THE SAME RANK AS GALAHAD OR EVEN A LITTLE STRONGER.

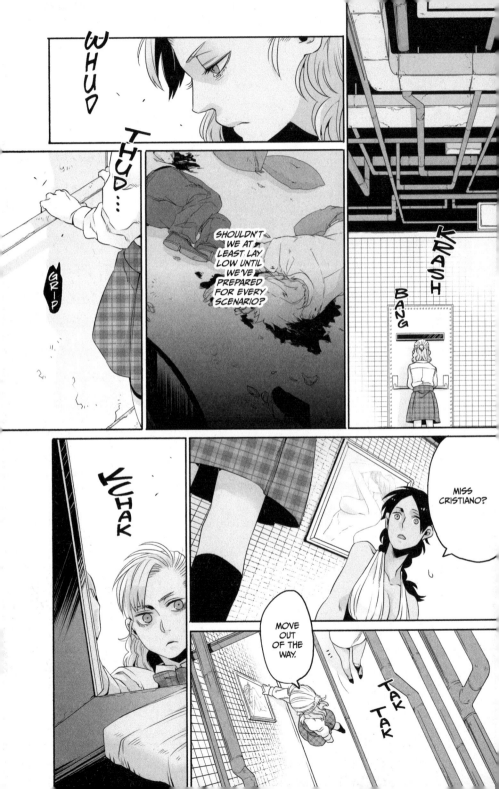

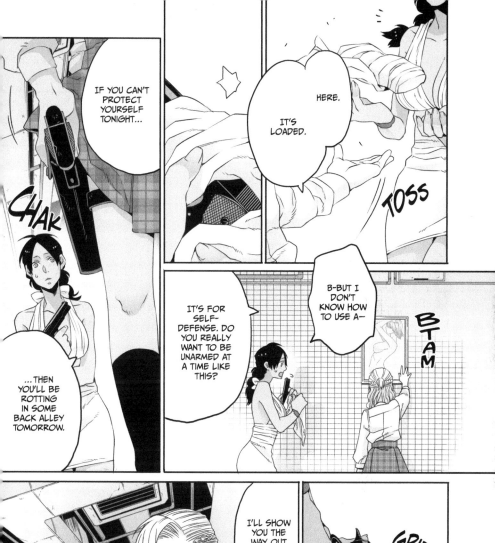

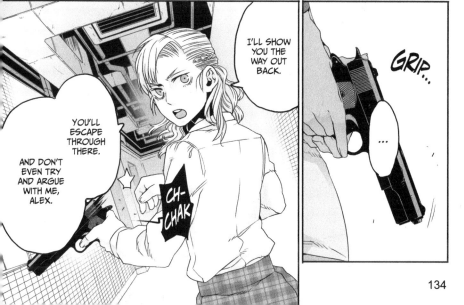

BUT WHAT ABOUT YOU?

NOBODY'S WATCHING. WHAT'S THE GOVERNMENT...

...DOING...

IT CAN'T BE.

URGH!

THERE'S NO WAY THAT BOY COULD HAVE DONE IT ON HIS OWN. WHICH MEANS...

HOW COULD THAT MANY OF THEM BE KILLED IN SO LITTLE TIME?

THERE WERE C AND B RANKS IN THAT GROUP.

DON'T! IT'S TOO DANGEROUS ON YOUR OWN!

THERE'S AN EMERGENCY EXIT UP AHEAD. GO THROUGH IT AND TAKE A LEFT OUT THE BACK ALLEY.

IT SHOULD PUT YOU IN THE DIRECTION WHERE THE HANDYMEN ARE.

WH...?

WAIT!

DASH

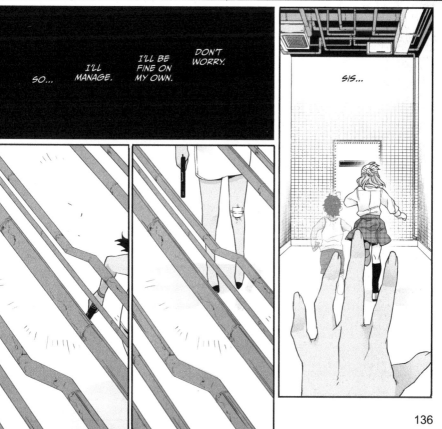

DON'T WORRY.

I'LL BE FINE ON MY OWN.

I'LL MANAGE.

SO...

SIS...

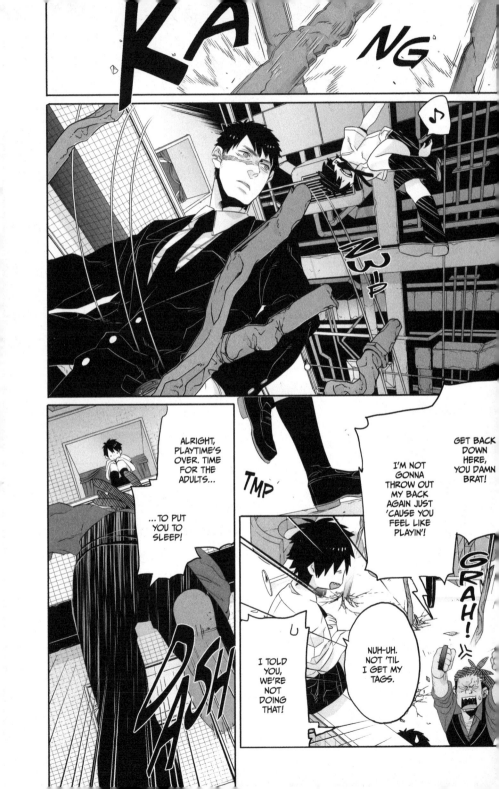

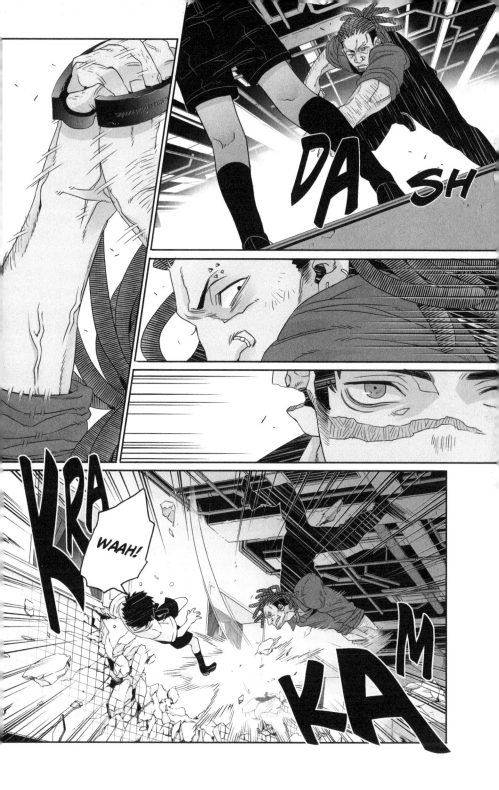

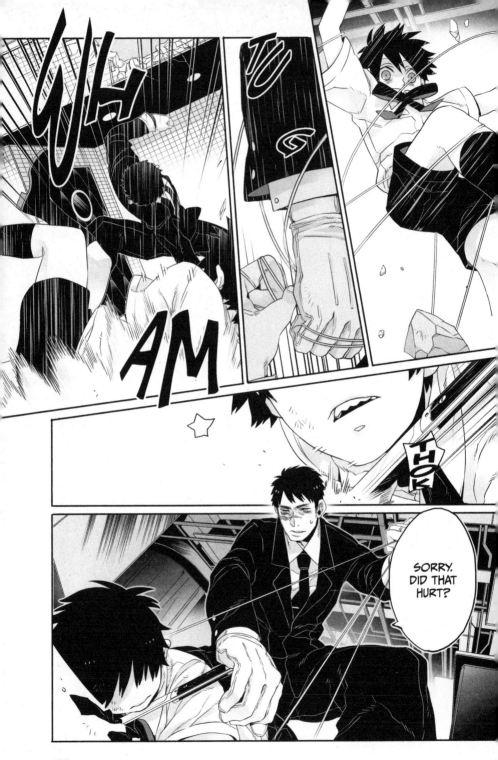

139

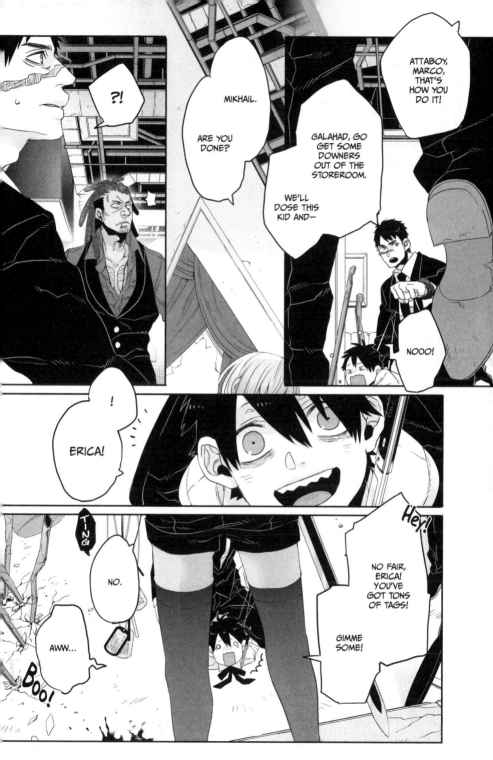

140

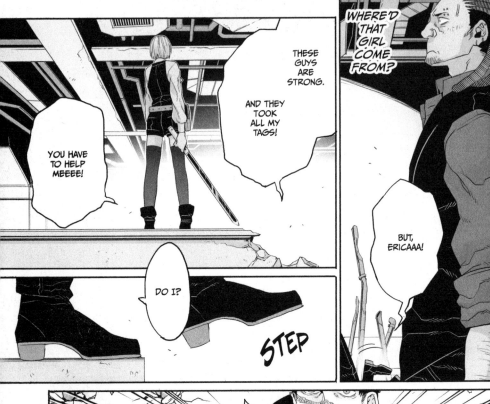

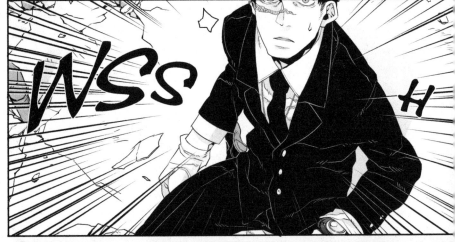

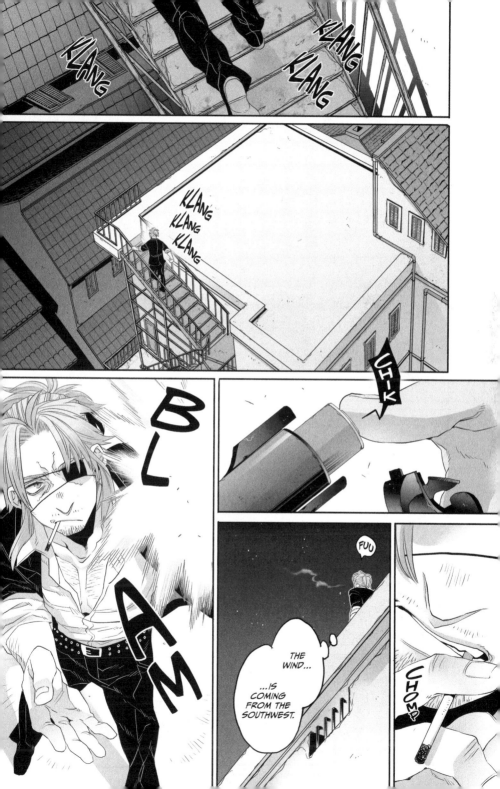

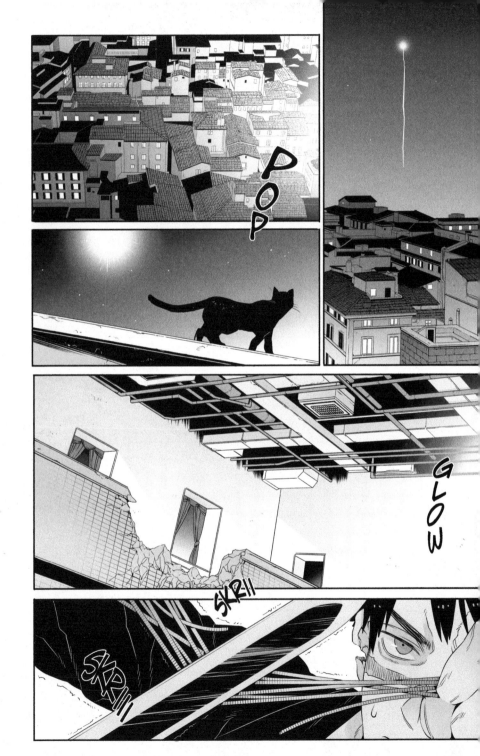

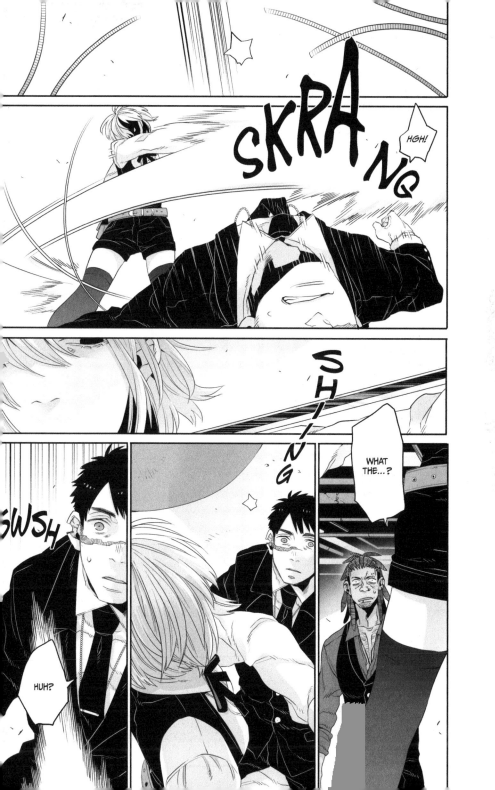

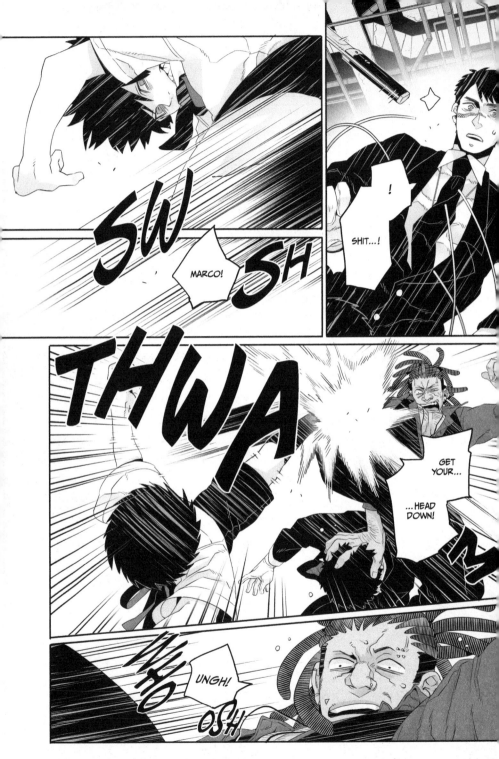

145

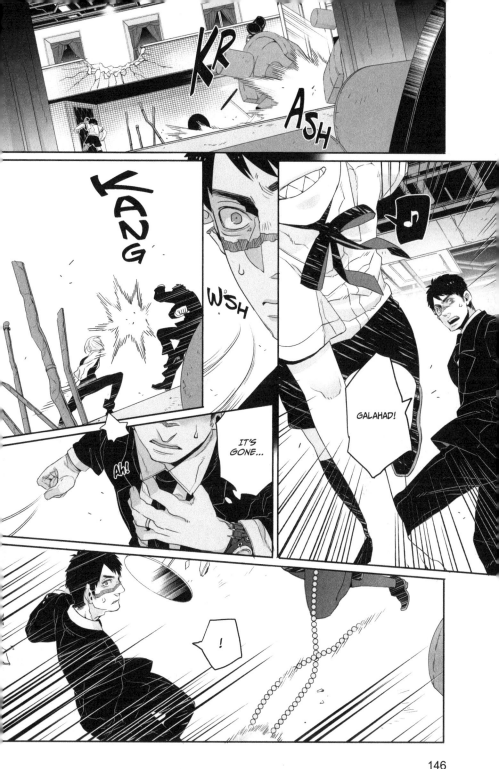

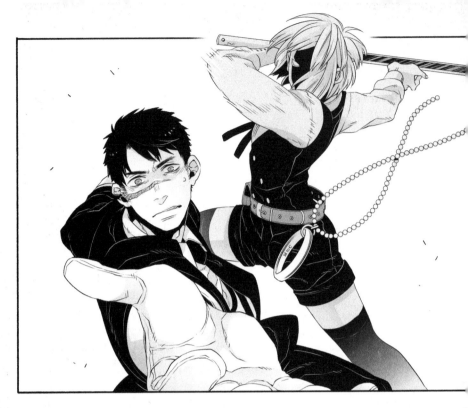

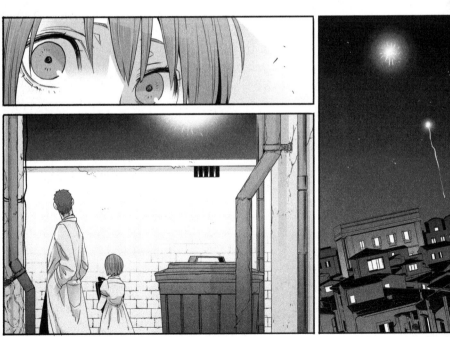

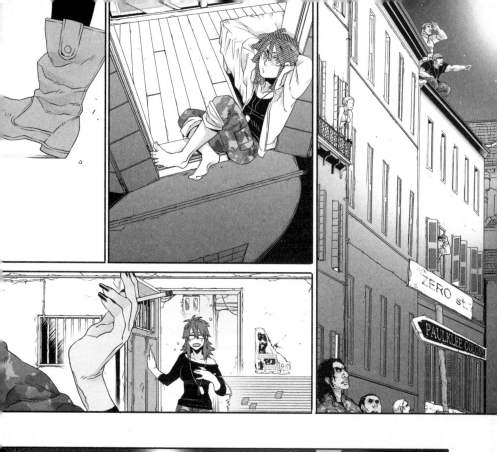

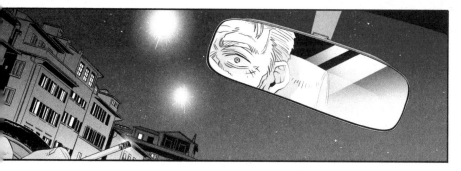

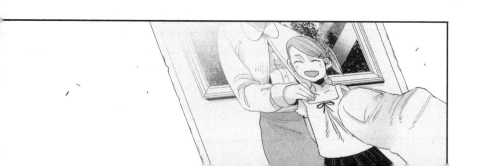

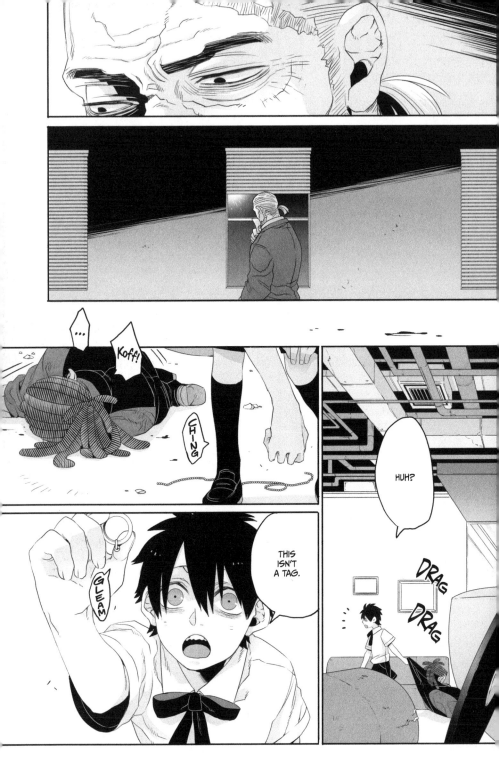

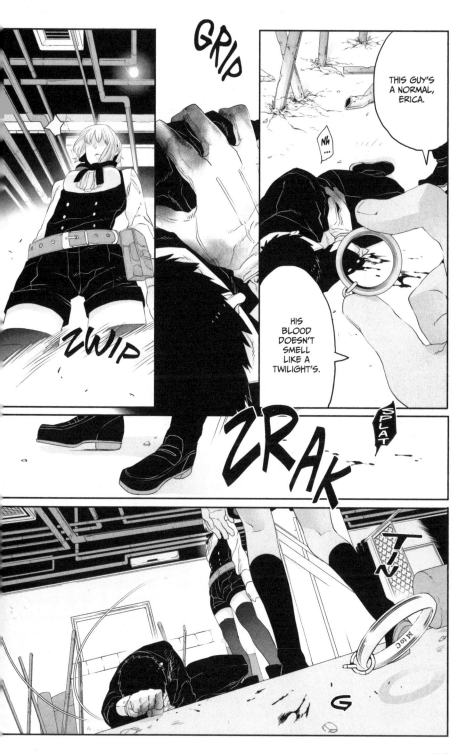

GET YOUR FILTHY HANDS OFF THAT.

YOU LITTLE PIECE OF SHIT!

...

HEY HEY, HOLD UP!

DON'T–

YOU GOT ME *DIRTY*...

...

... NGH.

KLINK

WH...?

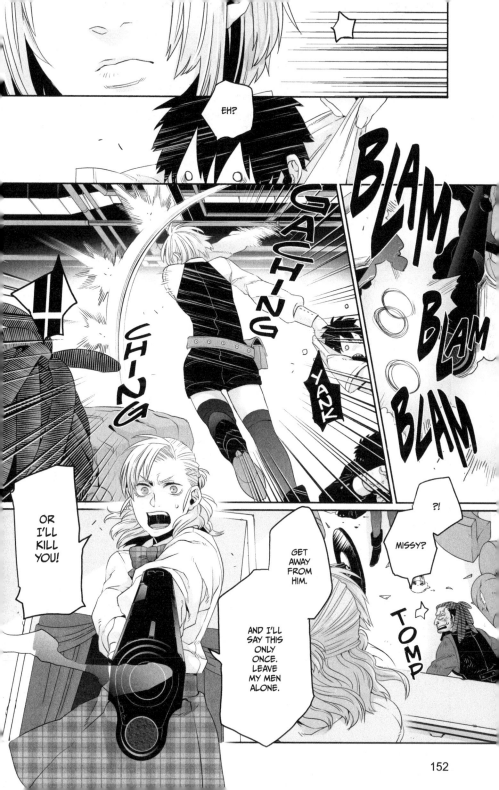

152

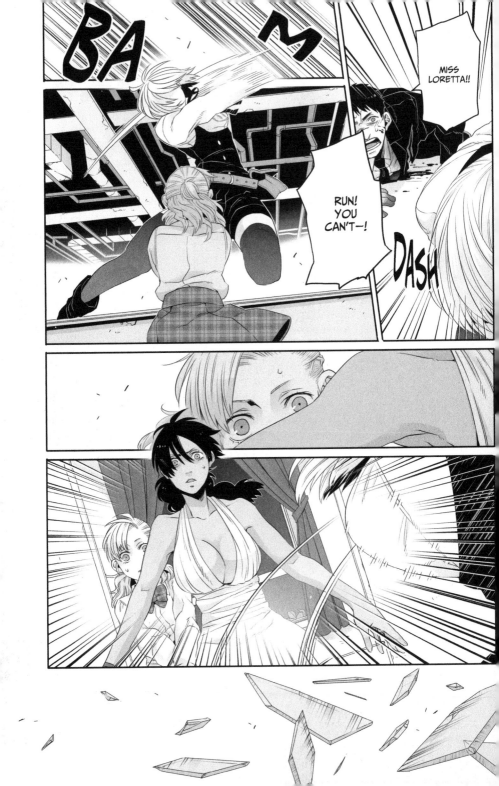

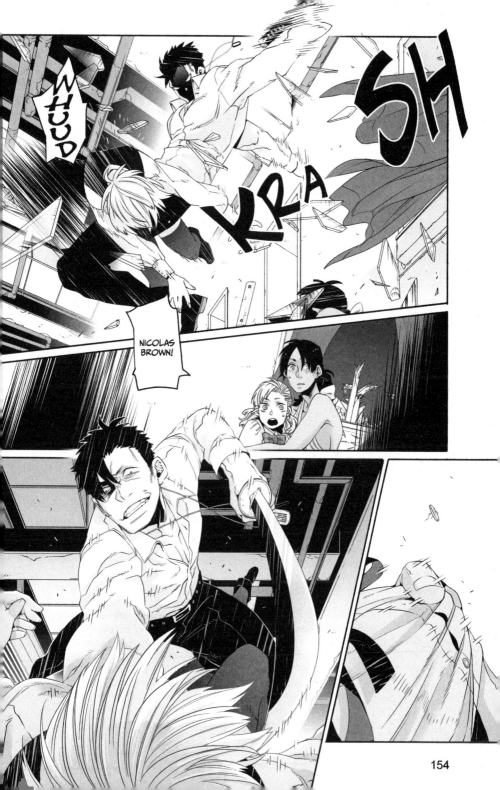

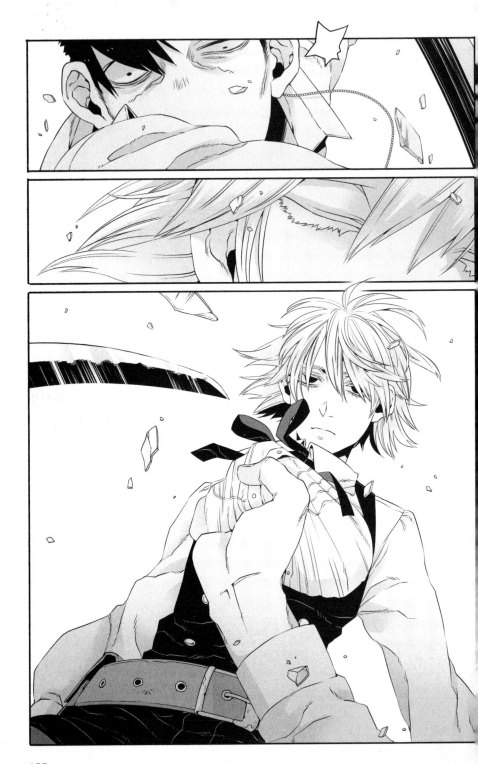

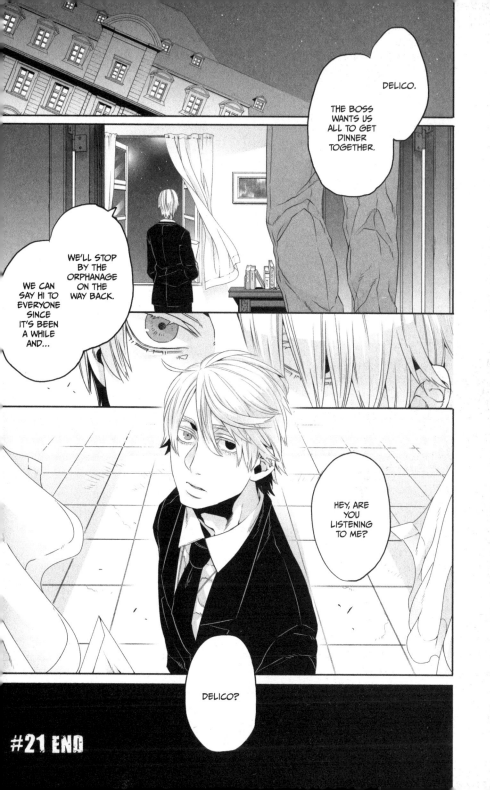

#21 END

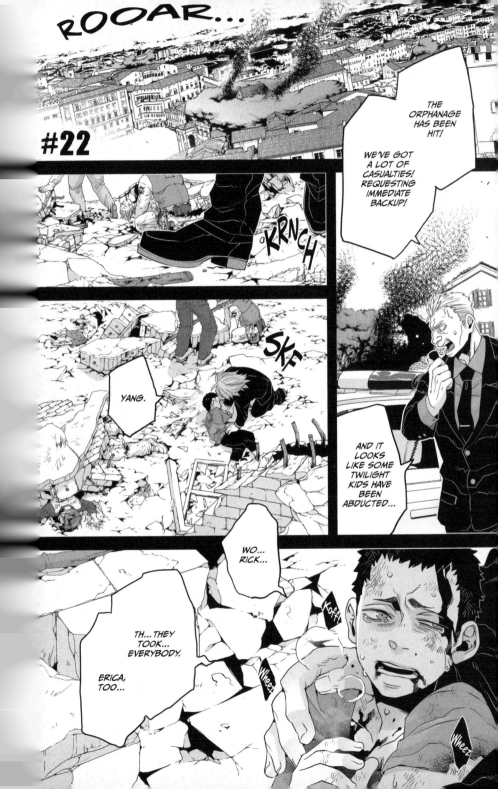

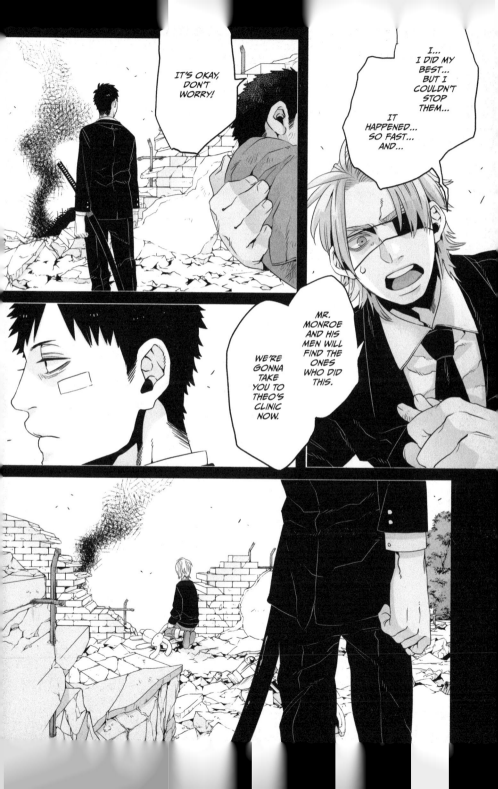

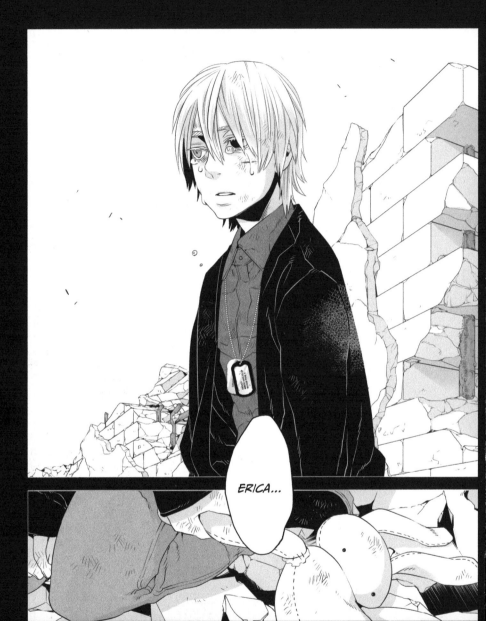

#22

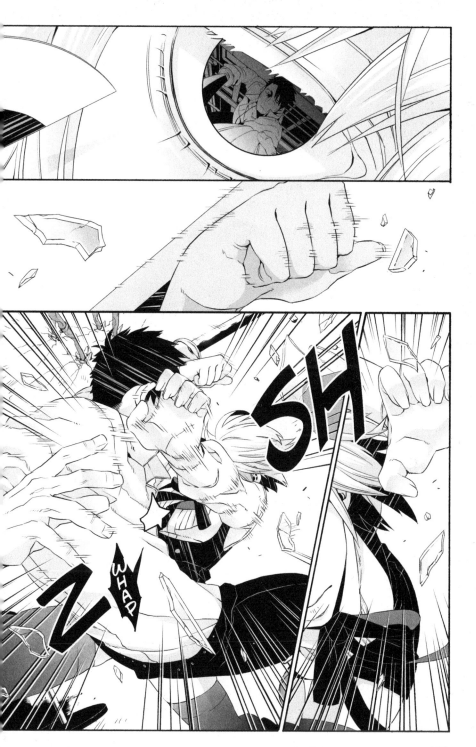

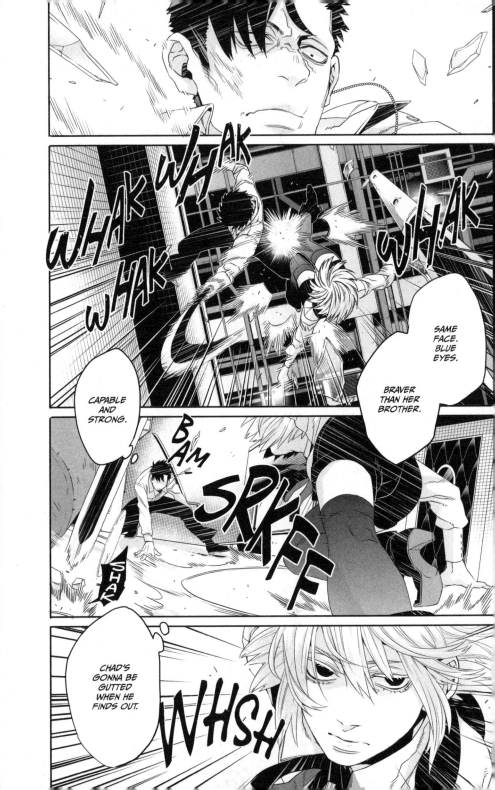

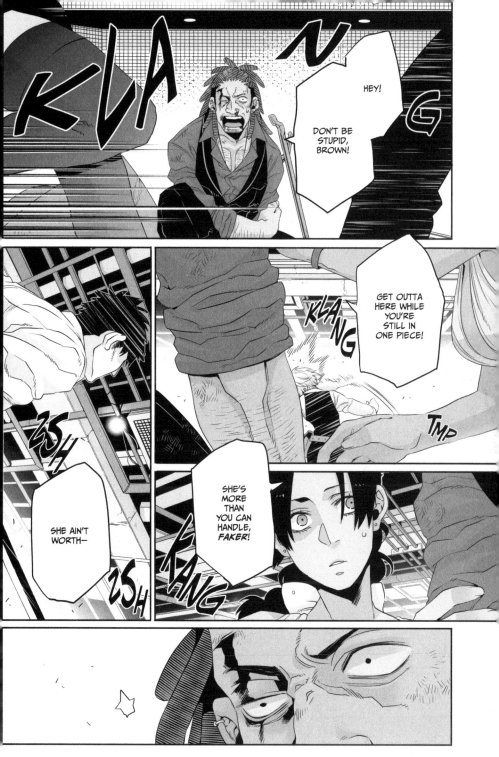

YOU TOO,
MISS
BENEDETTO.

TUG

!

BUT—

CHANG

SO THAT'S
HOW YOU
WANT IT TO
GO, HUH?

SHVR

WHAK

CHANG

LEAVE IT
TO NIC
FOR NOW.
COME
HELP ME!

CHANG
KHANG
CHANG

GALLY!

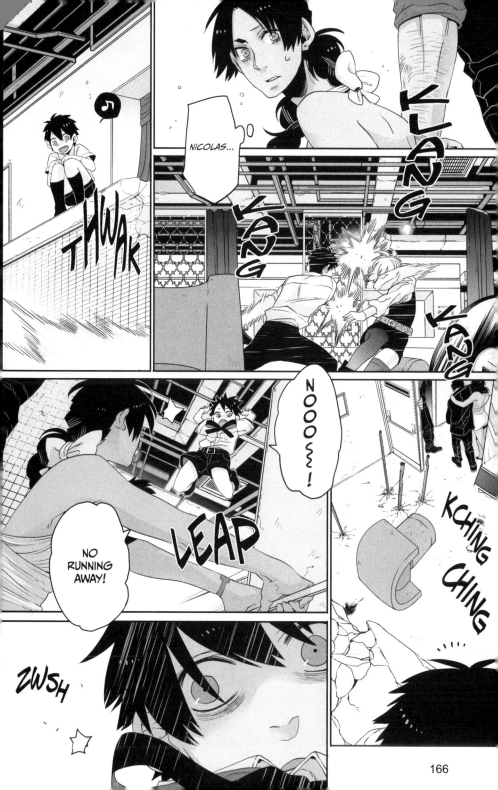

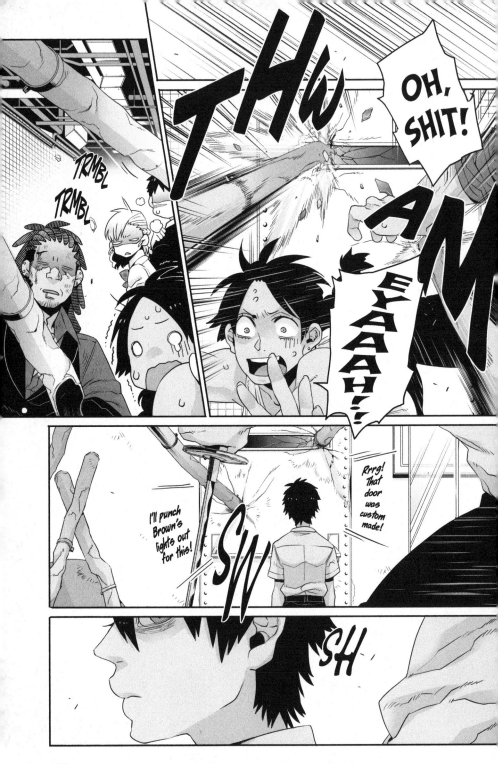

167

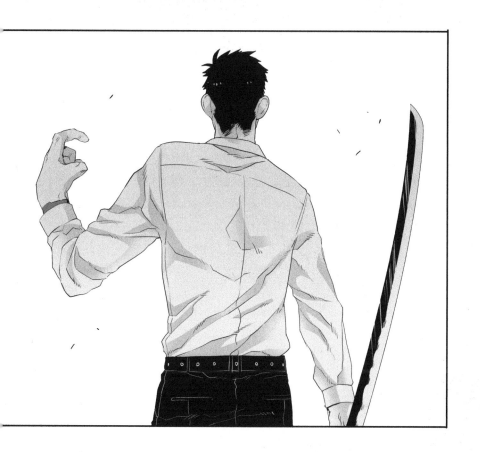

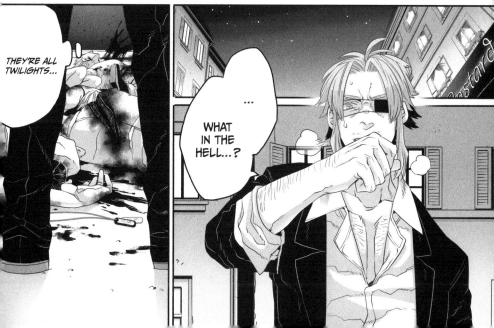

THEY'RE ALL
TWILIGHTS...

...

WHAT
IN THE
HELL...?

NO BLOOD ON IT, SO IT WASN'T ON ONE OF THE BODIES. WHICH MEANS...

...

GOD DAMN IT, NIC. YOU OVERDOSED AGAIN?

KLAN G

SH

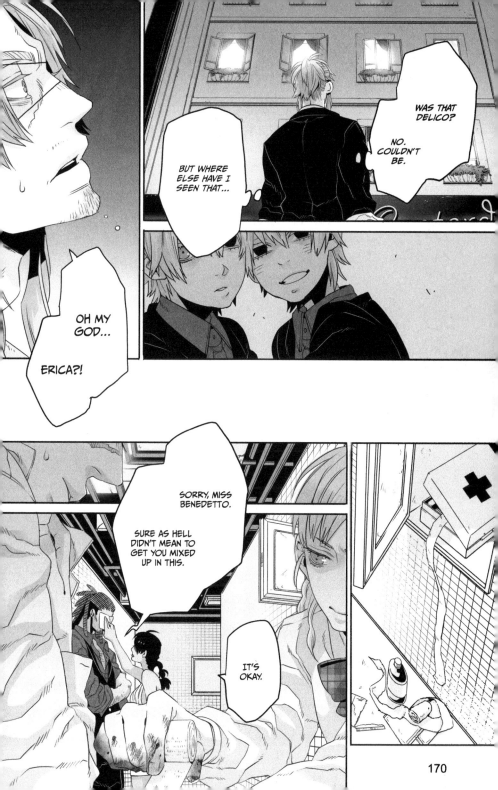

170

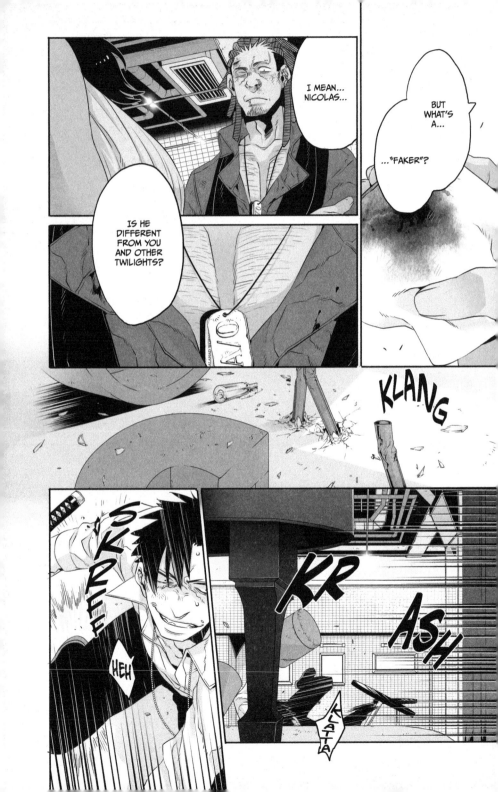

TWILIGHT RANKS ARE ASSIGNED ACCORDING TO PHYSICAL STRENGTH.

IN OTHER WORDS, THE STRONGER YOU GET, THE HIGHER YOUR RANK.

BUT HE'S DIFFERENT.

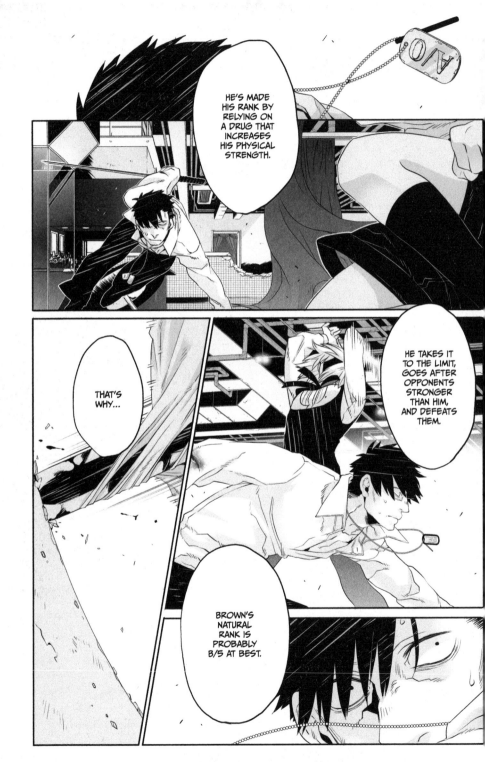

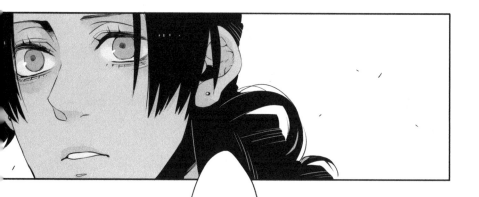

...HE'S A FAKER.

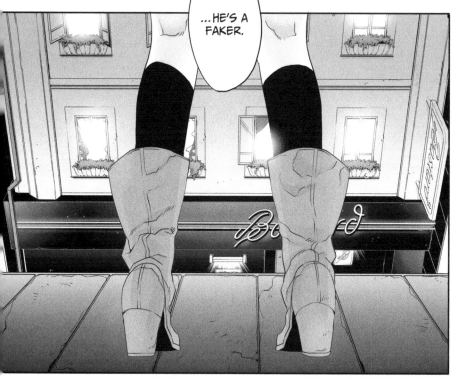

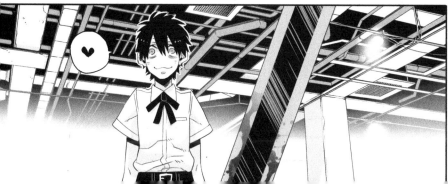

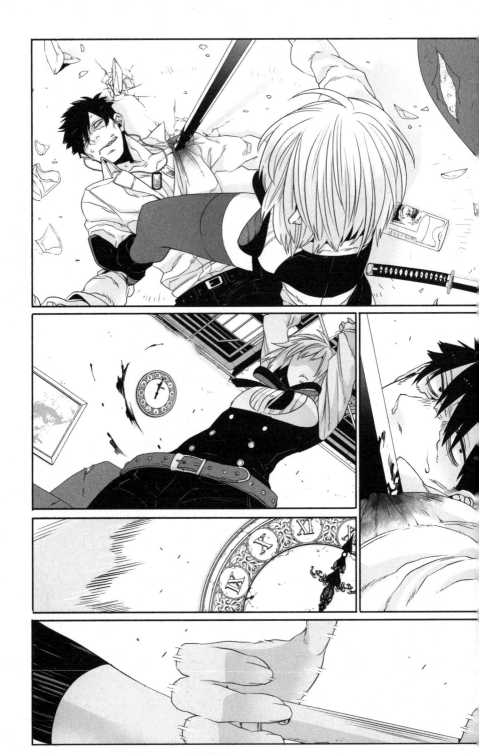

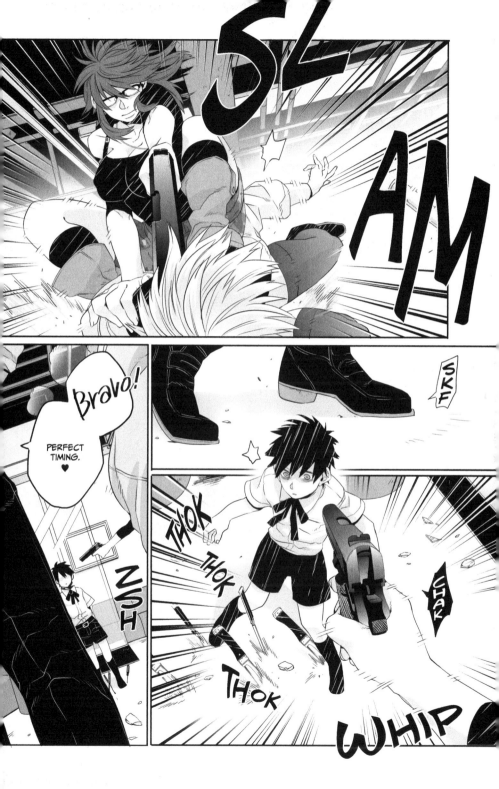

CHING

S/5 RANK...

GOOD THING THE GUILD LOOKOUTS SAW THAT EMERGENCY FLARE!

I KNEW PAULKLEE WOULD SEND YOU GUYS RIGHT OVER.

Phew!

DAMN, GINGER...

SLOW DOWN, WILL YA?!

YOU DON'T HAVE TO GO THAT FAST!

Huff!

Huff!

SWIP

I'VE SEEN YOUR FACE BEFORE.

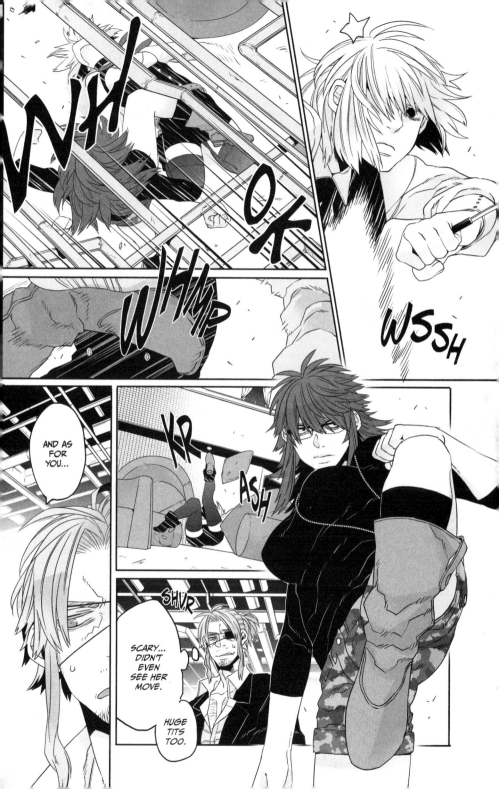

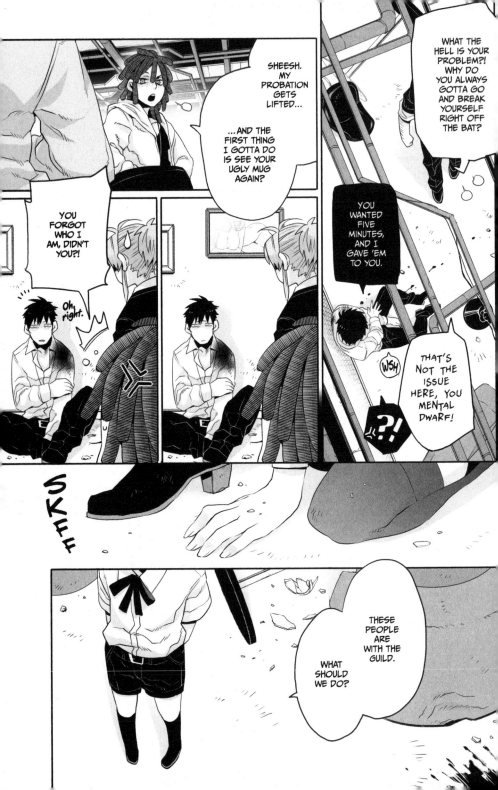

WEE-
OO

WEE-
OO

WEE-
OO

ERICA.

WEE-
OO WEE-
OO

WEE-
OO

THE SUSPECTS ARE STILL INSIDE WITH MISS CRISTIANO AND HER MEN!

SEAL THE EXITS!

SLAM SLAM

IS UNIT 3 HERE YET?

SQUEAL

THEY'RE TWO MINUTES OUT.

ANYONE WITHOUT AN ASSIGNED TASK SHOULD LOOK FOR SURVIVORS!

SLAM

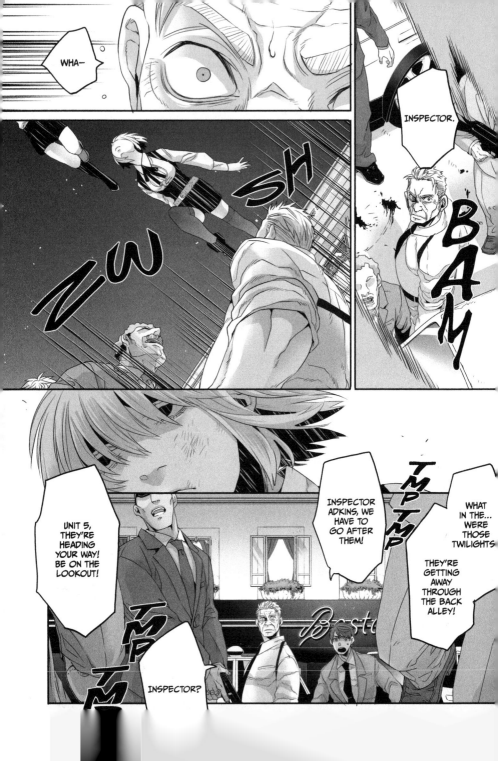

MARCO.

...

I GUESS THAT WAS A SILLY QUESTION.

DO *YOU* THINK YOU WERE WRONG, MISS?

DO YOU THINK I WAS WRONG?

182

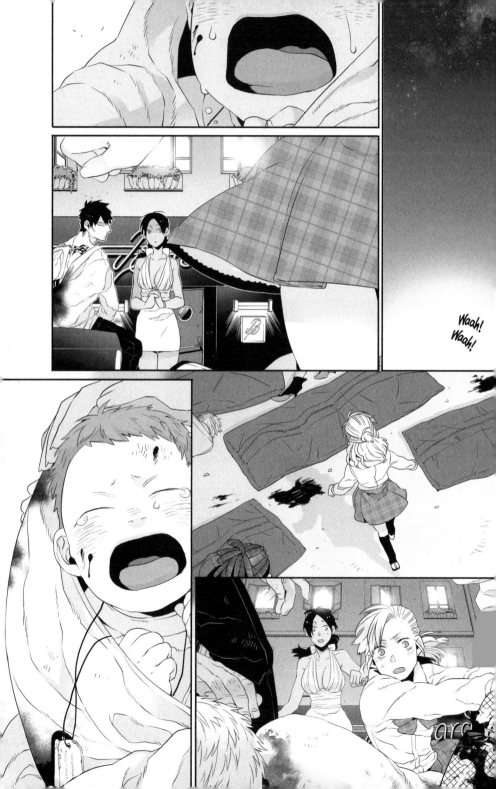

Waah!
Waah!

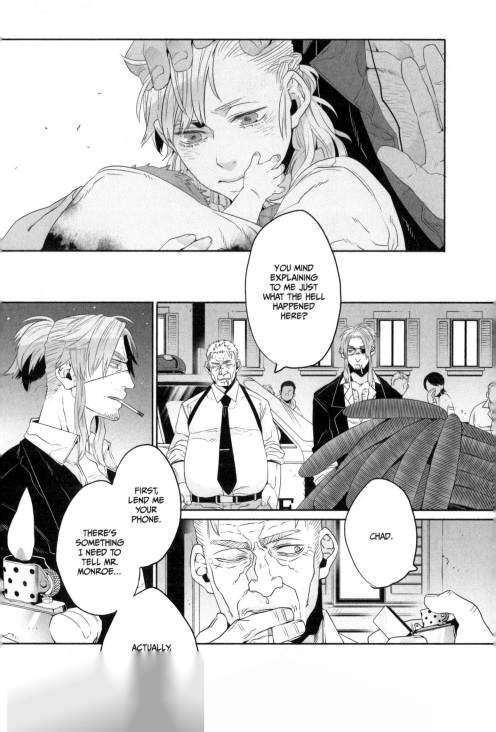

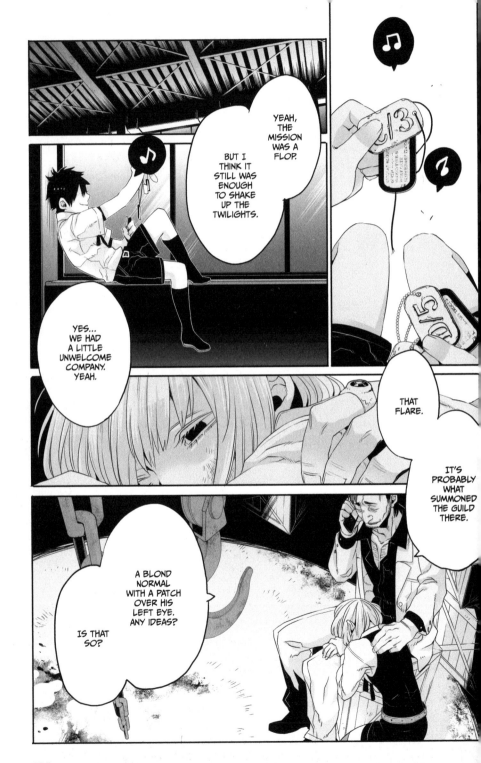

YES.

ESPECIALLY NOW THAT THE CORSICA FAMILY'S GOT *US*.

TOLD YA, MR. URANOS.

THERE WAS NO WAY THAT CHICK AND THE BRAT COULD DO IT.

HE'S STILL NOT HERE? THE LAST GUY?

I'M GETTING REALLY SICK OF WAITING FOR HIM.

THEY'RE USELESS. YOU SHOULD DROP 'EM.

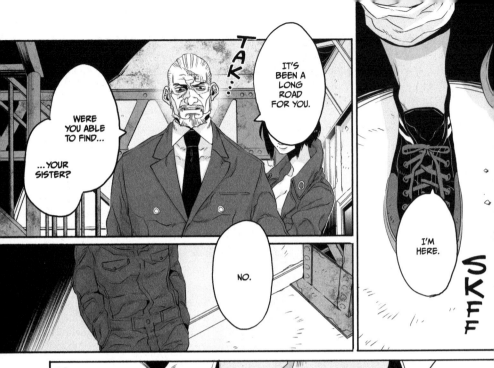

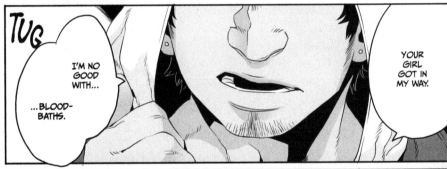

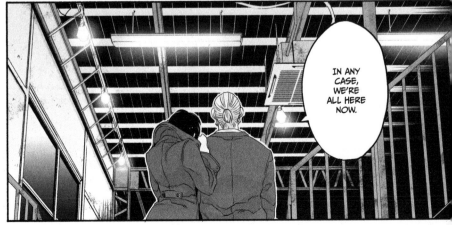

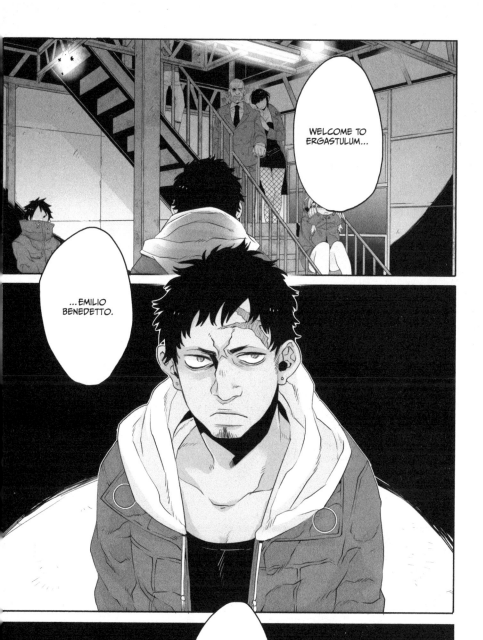

#22 END

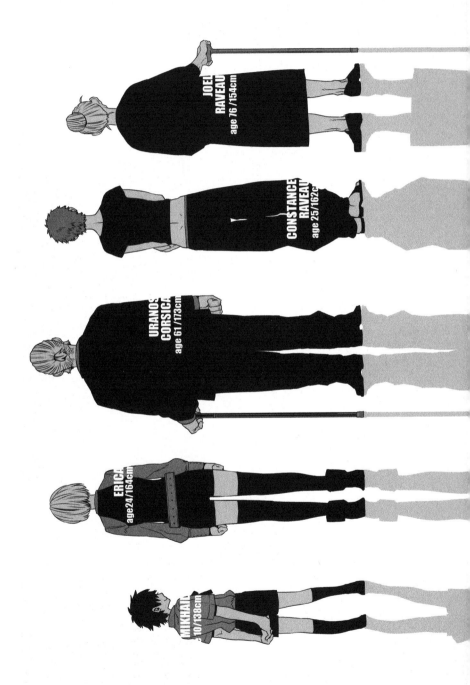

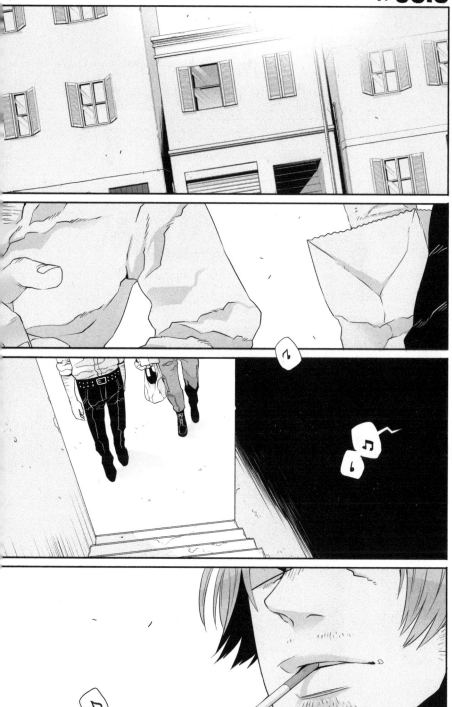

#06.5 END

Thank you again to: Mom / My Assistants Kamo, I, and H / Saimoto / Fumi / Editor H (honorary abbreviation)
Research assistance: JCN Mejiro Studio / Le Baron de Paris (honorary abbreviation)

IN THE NEXT VOLUME

The Hunters and the Destroyers continue to rampage through the city, toying with their prey and piling atrocity upon atrocity. With no time to mourn their fallen, the Paulklee Guild are forced to fend off their enemies' increasingly deadly attacks. The surviving members mobilize to fight back, and despite the terrible losses, hope is kept alive in the form of old vows honored and new ones made.

How to Draw Worick

①

② Draw a handsome face (comparatively speaking).

③ Draw hair.

④ Draw hair.

Done!

ABOUT THE AUTHOR

Kohske made her manga debut in 2009 with the short story "Postman" in *Shonen GanGan* magazine. Her first series, *Gangsta.*, began running in *Monthly Comic Bunch* in 2011 and became an instant hit. More about her work can be found on her website, http://gokohske.o-oi.net/.

GANGSTA.

Gangsta.
Volume 4

VIZ Signature Edition

Story & Art by Kohske

Translation & Adaptation/Katherine Schilling
Touch-up Art & Lettering/Eric Erbes
Cover & Graphic Design/Sam Elzway
Editor/Leyla Aker

The stories, characters and incidents mentioned in this
publication are entirely fictional.

Printed in the U.S.A.

Published by VIZ Media, LLC
P.O. Box 77010
San Francisco, CA 94107

10 9 8 7 6 5 4 3 2 1
First printing, November 2014

VIZ SIGNATURE

www.viz.com

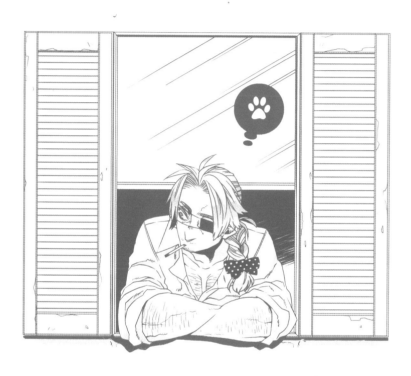

WHERE?

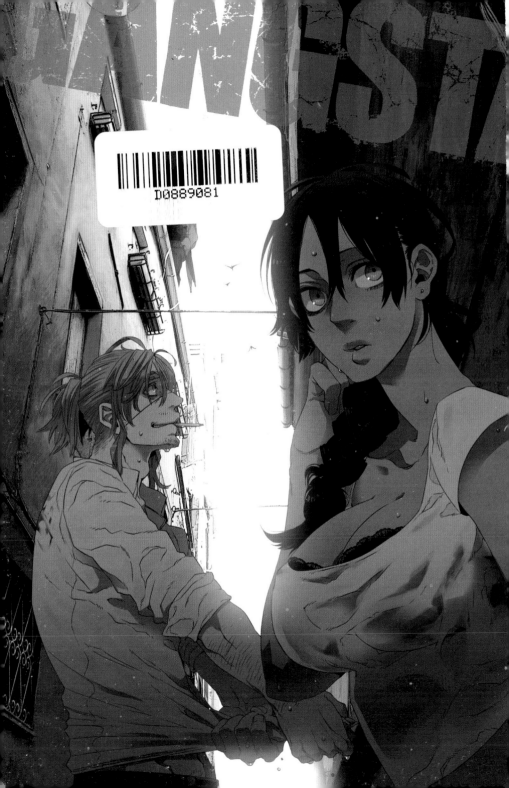